COSMOPOLITAN GREETINGS

By Allen Ginsberg

Poetry

Howl and Other Poems 1956
Kaddish and Other Poems 1961
Empty Mirror: Early Poems 1961
Reality Sandwiches 1963
Angkor Wat 1968
Planet News 1968
Airplane Dreams 1969
The Gates of Wrath: Rhymed Poems 1948–51 1972
The Fall of America: Poems of These States 1973
Iron Horse 1973
First Blues 1975
Mind Breaths: Poems 1971–76 1978
Plutonian Ode: Poems 1977–1980 1982
Collected Poems 1947–1980 1984
White Shroud: Poems 1980–1985 1986
Cosmopolitan Greetings: Poems 1986–1992 1994

Prose

The Yage Letters (WITH WILLIAM BURROUGHS) 1963
Indian Journals 1970
Gay Sunshine Interview (WITH ALLEN YOUNG) 1974
Allen Verbatim: Lectures on Poetry, Politics, Consciousness (GORDON BALL, ED.) 1974
Chicago Trial Testimony 1975
To Eberhart from Ginsberg 1976
Journals: Early Fifties, Early Sixties (GORDON BALL, ED.) 1977, 1993
As Ever: Collected Correspondence Allen Ginsberg & Neal Cassady
    (BARRY GIFFORD, ED.) 1977
Composed on the Tongue (Literary Conversations 1967–1977) 1980
Straight Hearts Delight, Love Poems and Selected Letters 1947–1980, with Peter
    Orlovsky (WINSTON LEYLAND, ED.) 1980
Howl, Original Draft Facsimile, Fully Annotated (BARRY MILES, ED.) 1986
The Visions of the Great Rememberer (with Visions of Cody, Jack Kerouac) 1993
Journals Mid-Fifties: 1954–1958 1995

Photography

Photographs (TWELVETREES PRESS) 1991
Snapshot Poetics (CHRONICLE BOOKS) 1993

Vocal Words and Music

First Blues CASSETTE TAPE ONLY (FOLKWAYS/SMITHSONIAN RECORDS FSS 37560) 1981
Howls, Raps & Roars 4 CD BOX (FANTASY) 1993
Hydrogen Jukebox (OPERA) WITH PHILIP GLASS, CD (ELEKTRA/NONESUCH) 1981
Holy Soul Jelly Roll: Poems & Songs 1949–1993 4 CD BOX (RHINO RECORDS) 1994

ALLEN GINSBERG

COSMOPOLITAN GREETINGS

POEMS

1986 - 1992

"I'm going to try speaking some reckless words,
and I want you to try to listen recklessly."

HarperPerennial

A Division of HarperCollins*Publishers*

Thanks to the hospitable editors, variants of these writings were printed first in: *After the Storm; Allen in Vision; Alpha Beat Soup; The Alternative Press; American Poetry Review; Be Released in Los Angeles; Big Scream; Big Sky; Black Box; Bombay Gin; Boulevard; Break the Mirror; Broadway 2; [Brooklyn College] English Majors Newsletter; Brooklyn Review; Casse Le Mirroir; City Lights Review; Collateral Damage; Collected Poems; Core; Cottonwood Commemorative; River City Portfolio 1987; Cover; Culturas; Entretien; Ergo; Esquire; Exit Zero; Exquisite Corps; Fall of America; Fear, Power; God* (recording); *First Blues; First Line; Flower Thief; Gandhabba; A Garden of Earthly Delight; Gathering of Poets; The Ginsberg Gallimaufry* (John Hammond Records); *Gown Literary Supplement; Grand Rapids College Review; Harper's; Holunderground; Howling Mantra; Hum Bom!* (broadside); *Hydrogen Jukebox* (libretto); *Inquiring Mind; Journal of the Gulf War; Karel Appel; Recent Work; Long Shot; Lovely Jobly; Man Alive!; Mill Street Forward; Moment; Moorish Science Monitor; Napalm Health Spa; Naropa Institute Summer Writing Program* (1991); *Nation; National Poetry Magazine of the Lower East Side; New Age Journal; New Censorship; A New Geography of Poets; New Letters; New Observations; New York Newsday; New York Planet; New York Times; Nigen Kazoku; Nightmares of Reason; Nola Express; La Nouvelle Chute de l'Amerique; Off the Wall; Organica; Paria; Pearl; Peckerwood; Personals Ad* (broadside); *Poem in the Form of a Snake* (broadside); *Poets for Life; Portable Lower East Side; Qualità di Tempo; Reality Sandwich; Riverrun; RubRoh!; Sekai; Semiotext[e]; Shambhala Sun; Sixpack; Steaua; Struga; Sugar, Alcohol & Meat* (recording); *Sulfur; Supplication for the Rebirth of the Vidyadhara Chögyam Trungpa, Rinpoche* (broadside); *Talus; Thinker Review* (broadside); *This Is Important; Threepenny Review; Tikkun; Underground Forest; Vagabond; Vajradhatu Sun; Venue; The Verdict Is In; Village Voice; Vinduet; Visiting Father & Friends* (pamphlet); *Vylizanej Mozek!; Washington Square News; Wiersze; World; WPFW 89.3 FM Poetry Anthology.*

A hardcover edition of this book was published in 1994 by HarperCollins Publishers.

COSMOPOLITAN GREETINGS: POEMS 1986–1992. Copyright © 1994 by Allen Ginsberg. All rights reserved. Printed in the United States of America. No part of this book may be used or reproduced in any manner whatsoever without written permission except in the case of brief quotations embodied in critical articles and reviews. For information address HarperCollins Publishers, Inc., 10 East 53rd Street, New York, NY 10022.

HarperCollins books may be purchased for educational, business, or sales promotional use. For information please write: Special Markets Department, HarperCollins Publishers, Inc., 10 East 53rd Street, New York, NY 10022.

First HarperPerennial edition published 1995.

Designed by Alma Hochhauser Orenstein

The Library of Congress has catalogued the hardcover edition as follows:

Ginsberg, Allen, 1926–
    Cosmopolitan greetings : poems, 1986–1992 / Allen Ginsberg.
      p.   cm.
    Includes index.
    ISBN 0-06-016770-X
    I. Title.
    PS3513.I74C67 1994
    811'.54   93-43627

ISBN 0-06-092623-6 (pbk.)

95 96 97 98 99 PS/RRD 10 9 8 7 6 5 4 3 2 1

To
Steven Taylor

If music be the food of love, play on.

CONTENTS

ACKNOWLEDGMENTS

Author wishes to inscribe grateful thanks to friends who've collaborated to type, track, edit, and critique *Cosmopolitan Greetings* thru a decade:

Harry Smith: Archetype cover design, typeface choice & logo.

Bill Morgan: Bibliographic lucidity.

Mark Ewert: Comix inspiration.

Bob Rosenthal: Holistic project supervision.

Steve Taylor: Musical guidance, lead sheets.

Regina Pellicano, Jacqueline Gens, Peter Hale, Steven Finbow, Victoria Smart, and Vicki Stanbury: Sympathetic meticulous assembly typescript text.

Andrew Wylie & Sarah Chalfant: Wise deadline protection.

Terry Karten and HarperCollins: Trustful & patient fidelity.

PREFACE

Improvisation in Beijing

I write poetry because the English word Inspiration comes from Latin
    Spiritus, breath, I want to breathe freely.

I write poetry because Walt Whitman gave world permission to speak
    with candor.

I write poetry because Walt Whitman opened up poetry's verse-line for
    unobstructed breath.

I write poetry because Ezra Pound saw an ivory tower, bet on one wrong
    horse, gave poets permission to write spoken vernacular idiom.

I write poetry because Pound pointed young Western poets to look at
    Chinese writing word pictures.

I write poetry because W. C. Williams living in Rutherford wrote New
    Jerseyesque "I kick yuh eye," asking, how measure that in iam-
    bic pentameter?

I write poetry because my father was poet my mother from Russia spoke
    Communist, died in a mad house.

I write poetry because young friend Gary Snyder sat to look at his
    thoughts as part of external phenomenal world just like a 1984
    conference table.

I write poetry because I suffer, born to die, kidneystones and high blood
    pressure, everybody suffers.

I write poetry because I suffer confusion not knowing what other people
    think.

I write because poetry can reveal my thoughts, cure my paranoia also
    other people's paranoia.

I write poetry because my mind wanders subject to sex politics Bud-
    dhadharma meditation.

I write poetry to make accurate picture my own mind.

I write poetry because I took Bodhisattva's Four Vows: Sentient creatures
    to liberate are numberless in the universe, my own greed anger

ignorance to cut thru's infinite, situations I find myself in are
countless as the sky okay, while awakened mind path's endless.

I write poetry because this morning I woke trembling with fear what
could I say in China?

I write poetry because Russian poets Mayakovsky and Yesenin commit-
ted suicide, somebody else has to talk.

I write poetry because my father reciting Shelley English poet & Vachel
Lindsay American poet out loud gave example—big wind inspiration breath.

I write poetry because writing sexual matters was censored in United
States.

I write poetry because millionaires East and West ride Rolls-Royce
limousines, poor people don't have enough money to fix their
teeth.

I write poetry because my genes and chromosomes fall in love with
young men not young women.

I write poetry because I have no dogmatic responsibility one day to the
next.

I write poetry because I want to be alone and want to talk to people.

I write poetry to talk back to Whitman, young people in ten years, talk
to old aunts and uncles still living near Newark, New Jersey.

I write poetry because I listened to black Blues on 1939 radio, Leadbelly
and Ma Rainey.

I write poetry inspired by youthful cheerful Beatles' songs grown old.

I write poetry because Chuang-tzu couldn't tell whether he was but-
terfly or man, Lao-tzu said water flows downhill, Confucius said
honor elders, I wanted to honor Whitman.

I write poetry because overgrazing sheep and cattle Mongolia to U.S.
Wild West destroys new grass & erosion creates deserts.

I write poetry wearing animal shoes.

I write poetry "First thought, best thought" always.

I write poetry because no ideas are comprehensible except as manifested
in minute particulars: "No ideas but in things."

I write poetry because the Tibetan Lama guru says, "Things are symbols
of themselves."

I write poetry because newspapers headline a black hole at our galaxy-
center, we're free to notice it.

I write poetry because World War I, World War II, nuclear bomb, and
  World War III if we want it, I don't need it.
I write poetry because first poem *Howl* not meant to be published was
  prosecuted by the police.
I write poetry because my second long poem *Kaddish* honored my
  mother's parinirvana in a mental hospital.
I write poetry because Hitler killed six million Jews, I'm Jewish.
I write poetry because Moscow said Stalin exiled 20 million Jews and
  intellectuals to Siberia, 15 million never came back to the Stray
  Dog Café, St. Petersburg.
I write poetry because I sing when I'm lonesome.
I write poetry because Walt Whitman said, "Do I contradict myself?
  Very well then I contradict myself (I am large, I contain multi-
  tudes.)"
I write poetry because my mind contradicts itself, one minute in New
  York, next minute the Dinaric Alps.
I write poetry because my head contains 10,000 thoughts.
I write poetry because no reason no because.
I write poetry because it's the best way to say everything in mind within
  6 minutes or a lifetime.

October 21, 1984

PROLOGUE

Visiting Father & Friends

I climbed the hillside to the lady's house.
There was Gregory, dressed as a velvet ape,
japing and laughing, elegant-handed, tumbling
somersaults and consulting with the hostess,
girls and wives familiar, feeding him like a baby.
He looked healthy, remarkable energy, up all night
talking jewelry, winding his watches, hair over his eyes,
jumping from one apartment to another.

Neal Cassady rosy-faced indifferent and affectionate
entertaining himself in company far from China
back in the USA old 1950s–1980s still kicking
his way thru the city, up Riverside Drive without a car.
He hugged me & turned attention to the night ladies
appearing disappearing in the bar, in apartments
and the street, his continued jackanapes wasting his time
& everyone else's but mysterious, maybe up to something
good—keep us all from committing more crimes,
political wars, or peace protests angrier than wars'
cannonball noises. He needed a place to sleep.

Then my father appeared, lone forlorn & healthy
still living by himself in an apartment a block up
the hill from Peter's ancient habitual pad, I hadn't
noticed where Louis lived these days, somehow obliterated
his home condition from my mind, took it for granted
tho never'd been curious enough to visit—but as I'd no place
to go tonight, & wonder'd why I'd not visited him recently,
I asked could I spend the night & bed down

there with him, his place had bedroom and bath
a giant Jewish residence apartment on Riverside Drive
refugees inhabited, driven away from Europe by Hitler,
where now my father lived—I entered, he showed me his couch
& told me get comfortable, I slept the night, but woke
when he shifted his sleeping pad closer to mine I got up
—he'd slept badly on a green inch-thick dusty
foam rubber plastic mattress I'd thrown out years ago,
poor cold mat upon the concrete cellar warehouse floor—
so that was it! He'd given his bed for my comfort!

No no I said, take back your bed, sleep comfortable
weary you deserve it, amazing you still get around,
I'm sorry I hadn't visited before, just didn't know
where you lived, here you are a block upstreet
from Peter, hospitable to me Neal & Gregory &
girlfriends of the night, old sweet Bohemian heart
don't sleep in the floor like that I'll take your place
on the mat & pass the night ok.
                              I went upstairs, happy to see
he had a place to lay his head for good, and woke in China.
Peter alive, though drinking a problem, Neal was dead
more years than my father Louis no longer
smiling alive, no wonder I'd not visited this place
he'd retired to a decade ago, How good to see him home, and take
his fatherly hospitality for granted among the living
and dead. Now wash my face, dress in my suit
on time for teaching classroom poetry at 8am Beijing,
far round the world away from Louis' grave in Jersey.

                              November 16, 1984, 6:52 A.M.
                              Baoding, P.R.C.

COSMOPOLITAN GREETINGS

You Don't Know It

In Russia the tyrant cockroach mustache ate 20 million souls
and you don't know it, you don't know it
In Czechoslovakia the police ate the feet of a generation that can't walk
and you don't know it, you don't know it
In Poland police state double agent cancer grew large as Catholic
        Church Frankenstein the state itself a Gulag Ship
and you don't know it, you don't know it
In Hungary tanks rolled over words of Politician Poets
and you don't know it
In Yugoslavia underground partisans of the Great Patriotic War
fought off the Great Patriotic Army of USSR
and you don't know it,

you know Tito but you don't know it

you say you don't know it these exiles from East Europe complaining
about someday Nicaragua Gulag

'cause you don't know it was the Writers Union intellectuals of Moscow
Vilnius Minsk Leningrad and Tbilisi

saying "Invade Immediately" their Curse on your Revolution

No you don't know it's not N.Y. Review of Books it's bohemian Krakow
Prague Budapest Belgrade E. Berlin

saying you don't know it you don't know it

Bella Akhmadulina in candlelight: "American poet you can never know
the tragedy of Russia"

Nor you General Borge Father Cardenal Vice President Rodríguez you
say you don't know it

Can't know it too busy with Yankee war Worse than memory of Stalin

That you know, yes you do know it

But you don't know it but you will know it

yes you will know it Lenin said

the first time History's Tragedy Second repeat it's Comedy

or was it Trotsky? Marx?

Non pasaran whispers from the Elbe, intellectual teeth chattering on
Danube & Vistula

Village churchbells drowned in Volga waters dammed by Commissar
engineers, riverwater evaporating faster than it reaches the sea

the Taiga woodsman weeping over "boring pamphlets" his forests pro-
vided

Kulaks rattling skulls & bones to seed a new millennial agriculture by
1980 '90 2000

with Lysenko's ectoplasm providing ammonia to grow Kasha

You don't know it intellectual Castro fat ass Power Chair a quarter
century

biting fairies' nuts off, sneaking into Manolo's desk to read my love
letters

making Heberto Padilla eat your speeches You don't know it's a frou-
frou among French intellectual magazines you glance at as vice
president of Nicaragua

between wars from North Yanquis and banquets with Pork & Rum after
        TV evening news—
                                        You don't know it
Madame Mandelstam's thick book's gossip, Mrs. Evgenia Ginzburg's
grey prisoners shitting on each other in the hull of the boat
on frozen sea out of Vladivostok going with the million
Card-carrying Party members old Bolshevik friends of Lenin
to the frozen puddles and hungry banks of Kolyma
where skeletons hit each other to keep alive you don't know it

And they don't know it, Aksionov Škvorecký Romain Rolland Ehren-
        burg Fedorenko Markov Yevtushenko—
don't know midnight Death Squad clubs on cobblestone no
the ears cut off, heads chopped open in Salvador don't know the million
Guatemala Indians in Model Villages—
Don't know 40,000 bellies ripped open by the d'Aubuisson hit-men for
        Born Again neoconservative Texans,
don't know Yanquis taking tea & 1916 money from the Douane, ex-
        change for Chinese opium
trading bananas to Europe for Tax Control in Managua & Shanghai—
don't know the holocaust in Salvador 25 years ago 30,000 shot one week
        for thinking Left-Pink-triangle yellow-red headband high on
        peyote
& you don't know Imagination that leaps like a frog in Communist
        Monastery Ponds—
Don't know you confess like a worm turning in a matchbox full of salt
Don't know Solitary, Lesbian Capo ordering Movie Star Princess to
        expose her ———
and her delicate pink ——— and her firm round ——— to the false
        dogs of Ideology Fart Yowp with big pricks Whip Blip Blip
        Blip—
Bugger it up in Dynamite Don't know the Marines in your mother's
        toilet
No you don't know it we don't know it only stupid American minstrels
        know intolerant gasbags ascending

with millions of Readers' Digest copies
and photo enlargements of a thumbnail translation of the Moravian
      Bible
Put in my shirt-pocket in a sweat eyes closing as the enemy approaches
to fall asleep & snore Don't I know it

January 25, 1986, 2:00–2:12 A.M.
Managua

On the Conduct of the World
Seeking Beauty Against Government

Is that the only way we can become like Indians, like Rhinoceri,
like Quartz Crystals, like organic farmers, live what we imagine
Adam & Eve to've been, caressing each other with trembling limbs
before the Snake of Revolutionary Sex wrapped itself round
the Tree of Knowledge? What would Roque Dalton joke about lately
teeth chattering like a machine gun as he debated mass tactics
with his Compañeros? Necessary to kill the Yanquis with big bomb
Yes but don't do it by yourself, better consult your mother
to get the Correct Line of Thought, if not consult Rimbaud once he got
       his leg cut off
or Lenin after his second stroke sending a message thru Mrs. Krupskaya
       to the rude Georgian, & just before his deathly fit when the
       Cheka aides outside
his door looked in coldly assuring him his affairs were in good hands
no need to move—What sickness at the pit of his stomach moved up to
       his brain?
What thought Khlebnikov on the hungry train exposing his stomach to
       the sun?
Or Mayakovsky before the bullet hit his brain, what sharp propaganda
       for action
on the Bureaucratic Battlefield in the Ministry of Collective Agriculture
       in Ukraine?
What Slogan for Futurist architects or epic hymn for masses of Com-
       munist Party Card holders in Futurity
on the conduct of the world seeking beauty against Government?

January 27, 1986

Hard Labor

After midnite, Second Avenue horseradish Beef
       at Kiev's wood tables—
The Kasha Mushrooms tastes good
       as Byelorussia usta when my momma
       ran away from Cossacks 1905
Did the 5 year plan work? How bad Stalin?
Am I a Stalinist? A Capitalist? A
       Bourgeois Stinker? A rotten Red?
No I'm a fairy with purple wings and white halo
       translucent as an onion ring in
the transsexual fluorescent light of Kiev
       Restaurant after a hard day's work

February 17, 1986, 12:35 A.M.

Velocity of Money

For Lee Berton

I'm delighted by the velocity of money as it whistles through windows of
      Lower East Side
Delighted skyscrapers rise grungy apartments fall on 84th Street's pave-
      ment
Delighted this year inflation drives me out on the street
with double digit interest rates in Capitalist worlds
I always was a communist, now we'll win
as usury makes walls thinner, books thicker & dumber
Usury makes my poetry more valuable
Manuscripts worth their weight in useless gold—
The velocity's what counts as the National Debt gets trillions higher
Everybody running after the rising dollar
Crowds of joggers down Broadway past City Hall on the way to the Fed
Nobody reads Dostoyevsky books anymore so they'll have to give
      passing ear
to my fragmented ravings in between President's speeches
Nothing's happening but the collapse of the Economy
so I can go back to sleep till the landlord wins his eviction suit in court

February 18, 1986, 10:00 A.M.

Sphincter

I hope my good old asshole holds out
60 years it's been mostly OK
Tho in Bolivia a fissure operation
       survived the *altiplano* hospital—
a little blood, no polyps, occasionally
       a small hemorrhoid
active, eager, receptive to phallus
       coke bottle, candle, carrot
       banana & fingers—
Now AIDS makes it shy, but still
       eager to serve—
out with the dumps, in with the condom'd
       orgasmic friend—
still rubbery muscular,
       unashamed wide open for joy
But another 20 years who knows,
       old folks got troubles everywhere—
necks, prostates, stomachs, joints—
       Hope the old hole stays young
       till death, relax

March 15, 1986, 1:00 P.M.

Spot Anger

"Drive all blames into one"

Allen when you get angry you got two choices—
Konk your head on the floor with words
Bang the kitchen table, slap taxicab doors,
        insult hotel toilets
Snarl into National microphones, sneer at the
        speedfreak closet girl syringiste—
Why not more subtle, grab your anger by the wings
and bag it in the garbage pail
Look around by the venetian blind
It's only you in the universe's kitchen—
A subtler wave of the hand, patience—
Say, I don't want this Saturn trip, no thanks,
Domo arigato how nice but I'll not entertain
        Dr. Frankenstein till Monday
These pants don't fit, may I borrow your library card—
Breathe your typhoonic tantrum in, exhale a gentle
        breath of Ginsberg out the kitchen window
wafting a Springtime Fairy feather-slight
        raising a big iron pipe
to konk Mr. Temper Tantrum on his green bull noodle & fly off
over Manhattan weaving silver laughter
        round skyscraper spires.

April 24, 1986, 6:00 A.M.

London Dream Doors

On London's Tavern's wooden table, been reading Kit Smart—
God sent him to sea for pearls—till eyes heavy must sleep—
So went upstairs to my boardinghouse room yet the tall dark
boy that lived across the hall'd just got under covers
in a high Captain's bed, but left his door wide open,
his room furnished mahogany, oak crowded to the closets—
I gazed alas he was handsome, older than my choice of flesh
smooth boyhood, the lad had dark eyes, long limbs
a little hair on legs and chest, a little beard and smile—
I dozed, woke and returned from the bog, again passing
his room at stairtop— He lay in bed eyes open, I paused—
then turned aside thru his door, an embrace before going
to sleep in my own solid room I'd rented, first night
in this odd town, I'd come to teach a few strangers Love
& Poetry— So cast myself on his chest for a hug goodnight,
a second's surprise like father-son sweet dreams—
He clasped arms around me, held tight, I stopped a second—
More than I'd hoped for! Refreshing friendliness!—
lay there a minute, his warmth remained, spontaneous—
Grateful hugged his chest & quickly kissed his neck
& face, haste before I must rise— Yet no need to go
so with right leg I pushed the door in, closed,
we were alone. He pulled me on top of him, held each other,
I passed my hand along his side down to his thigh
he shivered, hands on my back, we began to sweat
under covers, his skin like slippery meat, the heat
of our embrace familiar, companionable surprise, I was
to be loved by his strong form, how soon hug his middle?
touch his flaccid glans? My own already thick with pleasure—
chest to his chest, legs intertwined, hard hair felt
uncomfortable under my hand—moved my palm across
his slimy stomach, sweat not unpleasant, close heat
amazed us both, secret freedom in his antique room,
invitation to explore night's pleasure, fresh conscience,

muscled thoughts, hearts glowing astounded happiness a brief
8 hours in the dark— What to do? I kissed his solar plexus
& belly above loins, he sighed and breathed on my neck in back,
affectionate clasped to his breast, arm round my waist— eyes
closed I lay still, head under white muslin in dim light,
quilt set aside for the heat—

                The door opened suddenly!
"You'll have to pay for the night's furniture" announced
the landlord. "You'll have to pay for the sink water and extra
covers! We rent or sell!" He fell silent. Hadn't he noticed
my bulk under thin sheet-cloth? But next instant he was
gone downstairs to write up the bill, door left ajar.
"Into my closet!" my new friend whispered urgent, "the first door!"—
The knob on his mirrored armoire stuck, wouldn't open,
same horrific closet of old play-movie nightmare blackouts—I saw
my own room entrance across the hall—"I'll go in there, seconds
to hide," fast before the old fellow returns! Naked trailing
sheet & blanket I crossed the hall stealthy, closed my bedroom
door behind, just time enough? Alas bed sheets blocked
the door jamb, clogged the landing, pull them through, I strained,
dragged awkward blankets inside in a trice and woke under
springtime sheets and linen cover alone, East Twelfth Street,
last night with Bengali Marathi Urdu poets, Museum of Modern Art.

May 6, 1986, 3:10 A.M.

Cosmopolitan Greetings

*To Struga Festival Golden Wreath Laureates
& International Bards 1986*

Stand up against governments, against God.

Stay irresponsible.

Say only what we know & imagine.

Absolutes are coercion.

Change is absolute.

Ordinary mind includes eternal perceptions.

Observe what's vivid.

Notice what you notice.

Catch yourself thinking.

Vividness is self-selecting.

If we don't show anyone, we're free to write anything.

Remember the future.

Advise only yourself.

Don't drink yourself to death.

Two molecules clanking against each other require an observer to
become scientific data.

The measuring instrument determines the appearance of the
phenomenal world after Einstein.

The universe is subjective.

Walt Whitman celebrated Person.

We are observer, measuring instrument, eye, subject, Person.

Universe is Person.

Inside skull vast as outside skull.

Mind is outer space.

"Each on his bed spoke to himself alone, making no sound."

"First thought, best thought."

Mind is shapely, Art is shapely.

Maximum information, minimum number of syllables.

Syntax condensed, sound is solid.

Intense fragments of spoken idiom, best.

Consonants around vowels make sense.

Savor vowels, appreciate consonants.

Subject is known by what she sees.

Others can measure their vision by what we see.

Candor ends paranoia.

Kral Majales
June 25, 1986
Boulder, Colorado

FIFTH INTERNATIONALE

A- rise Ye Prisoners of your mind-Set A- rise Neu-ro-tics of the

Earth For In- sight thunders Li-ber- a - tion A Sac-red world's in

Birth. No more At-tach-ment's chains bind us Minds Ag-

-res-sion no more rules The Earth shall rise on New foun-

-da- tions We have been jerks we shall be Fools 'Tis the

Path of Ac-cu- mu- la- tion Let each sit on his place The

In- ter- national Crazy Wis- dom School Could

save the Hu — man Race.

Fifth Internationale

To Billy MacKeever

Arise ye prisoners of your mind-set
Arise Neurotics of the Earth
For Insight thunders Liberation
A sacred world's in birth

No more Attachment's chains shall bind us
Mind's Aggression no more rules
The Earth shall rise on new foundations
We have been jerks we shall be Fools

'Tis the Path of Accumulation
Let each sit on his place
The International Crazy Wisdom School
Could save the Human Race

July 1986
Naropa

EUROPE, WHO KNOWS?

All o-ver Eu-rope people are saying "Who knows?" "Who knows?" As-pho-del's fine but next year what comes with the rose?

LAST STANZA

Cab-bage smells good but de- pends which way the wind blows

All o-ver Europe people are saying "Who knows?" "Who knows?"

If we didn't eat poison we'd starve Brother, ev'ry one knows.

Europe, Who Knows?

All over Europe people are saying, "Who knows?"
Asphodel's fine but next year what comes with the rose?
Cabbage smells good but depends which way the wind blows
All over Europe people are saying, "Who knows?"

Wormwood skies'll poison the sea: *Revelation*
Oslo to Athens black clouds've enlightened the nations
Cesium mushrooms & milk may mutate the Creation
All over Europe people are saying, "Who knows?"

Crossing the park in Munich Max Planck Institute
On my forearm and brow a film of invisible soot
Fell on my skin out of heaven, a new set of clothes
All over Europe people are saying, "Who knows?"

Woke up in Poland, maple leaves just wilted down
Not a cloud in the sky inexplicably cold on the ground
Kids in the yard were playing without any clothes
All over Europe people are saying, "Who knows?"

Phoned up the doctor, official reply: "Never mind"
Same afternoon suggested we take iodine
Three days later Chernobyl's error disclosed
All over Europe people are saying, "Who knows?"

Slaughtered the reindeer in Lapland, Lapps on the dole
Camembert radioactive, in Zurich, the gold
In the Cotswolds of England all the sheep markets were closed
All over Europe people are saying, "Who knows?"

If a liter of water's one x-ray in Washington State
So in milk bars of Minsk what does it cost a milkshake?
Big apples this year, we still have to eat up what grows
If we didn't eat poison we'd starve, Brother, everyone knows.

September 12, 1986 (with Steven Taylor)
Warsaw Airport

Graphic Winces

In highschool when you crack your front tooth bending down too fast
   over the porcelain water fountain
or raise the tuna sandwich to your open mouth and a cockroach tickles
   your knuckle
or step off the kitchen cabinet ladder on the ball of your foot hear the
   piercing meow of a soft kitten
or sit on a rattling subway next the woman scratching sores on her legs,
   thick pus on her fingers
or put your tongue to a winter-frozen porch door, a layer of frightening
   white flesh sticks to the wooden frame—
or pinch your little baby boy's fat neck skin in the last teeth of his
   snowsuit zipper
or when you cross Route 85 the double yellow line's painted over a dead
   possum
or tip your stale party Budweiser on the windowsill to your lips, taste
   Marlboro butts floating top of the can—
or fighting on the second flight of the tenement push your younger
   sister down the marble stairs she bites her tongue in half, they
   have to sew it back in the hospital—
or at icebox grabbing the half-eaten Nestlé's Crunch a sliver of foil
   sparks on your back molar's silver filling
or playing dare in High School you fall legs split on opposite sides of a
   high iron spiked fence
or kicked in the Karate Dojo hear the sound like a cracked twig then feel
   a slow dull throb in your left forearm,
or tripping fall on the sidewalk & rip last week's scab off your left knee
You might grimace, a sharp breath from the solar plexus, chill spreading
   from shoulderblades and down the arms,
or you may wince, tingling twixt sphincter and scrotum a subtle electric
   discharge.

December 8, 1986

Imitation of K.S.

The young kid, horror buff, monster Commissar, ghoul connoisseur, attic bedroom postered with violet skulls, cigarette butts on the floor, thinks he'd strangle girls after orgasm—pumping iron 13 years old, 175-pound muscleman, his father shot at him, missed, hit the door, he saw his mother's tiny apron, father clutched his throat, six foot four drunk, today's in Alcohol Anonymous. Even eyes, symmetric face, aged twenty, acid-free-plastic packages of *Ghoul Ghosts*, *Monsters Nowhere*, *Evil Demons of the Dead*, *Frenzy Reanimator*, *Psycho Nightmare on Elm Street* stacked by his mattress; he followed me around, carried my harmonium box, protected me from the drunk Tibetan, came to my bed; head on his shoulder, I felt his naked heart, "my Cock's half dead," he thinks he'll cut it off, can't stand to be touched, never touches himself, iron legs, "skinny dynamite," thick biceps, a six-day black fuzz on his even jaw, shining eyes, "I love you too."

March 22, 1987

I Went to the Movie of Life

In the mud, in the night, in Mississippi Delta roads
outside Clarksdale I slogged along Lights flashed
under trees, my black companion motioned "Here they are,
your company."—Like giant rhinoceri with painted faces
splashed all over side and snout, headlights glaring in rain,
one after another buses rolled past us toward Book Hotel
Boarding House, up the hill, town ahead.
                                        Accompanying me, two girls
pitched in the dark slush garbaged road, slipping in deep ruts
wheels'd left behind sucking at their high heels, staining granny
dresses sequined magic marked with astral signs, Head groupies
who knew the way to this Grateful Dead half-century heroes'
caravan pit stop for the night. I climbed mid-road, a toad
hopped before my foot, I shrank aside, unthinking'd kicked it off
with leather shoe, animal feet scurried back at my sight—
a little monster on his back bled red, nearby this prey a lizard
with large eyes retreated, and a rat curled tail and slithered
in mud wet to the dirt gutter, repelled. A long climb ahead, the girls'd
make it or not, I moved on, eager to rejoin old company.
Merry Pranksters with aged pride in peacock-feathered beds,
shining mylar mirror-paper walls, acid mothers with strobe-lit radios,
long-haired men, gaunt 60s' Diggers emerged from the night
to rest, bathe, cook spaghetti, nurse their kids,
smoke pipes and squat with Indian sages round charcoal
braziers in their cars; profound American dreamers,
I was in their company again after long years, byways
alone looking for lovers in bar street country towns
and sunlit cities, rain & shine, snow & spring-bud backyard
brick walls, ominous adventures behind the Iron Curtain.
Were we all grown old? I looked for my late boyfriends,
dancing to Electric Blues with their guns and smoke round jukebox walls
the smell of hash and country ham, old newspaper media stars
wandering room after room: Pentagon refugee Ellsberg, old dove

Dellinger bathing in an iron tub with a patch in his stomach wall
Abbie Hoffman explaining the natural strategy of city political saint
works, Quicksilver Messenger musicians, Berkeley orators
with half-grown children in their sox & dirty faces, alcohol
uncles who played chess & strummed banjos frayed by broken
fingernails.
    Where's Ken Kesey, away tonite in another megalopolis hosting
hypnosis parties for Hell's Angels, maybe nail them down on stage
or radio, Neal must be tending his daughters in Los Gatos,
pacifying his wife, coming down amphetamines in his bedroom,
or downers to sleep this night away & wake for work
in the great Bay Carnival tented among smokestacks, railroad
tracks and freeways under box-house urban hills.
Young movie stars with grizzled beards passed thru bus corridors
looking for Dylan in the movie office, re-swaggering old roles,
recorded words now sung in Leningrad and Shanghai, their wives
in tortoise shell glasses & paisley shawls & towels tending
cauldrons bubbling with spaghetti sauce & racks of venison,
squirrel or lamb; ovens open with hot rhubarb pies—
Who should I love? Here one with leather hat, blond hair
strong body middle age, face frowned in awful thought,
beer in hand by the bathroom wall? That Digger boy I knew
with giant phallos, bald head studying medicine walked by,
preoccupied with anatomy homework, rolling a joint, his
thick fingers at his chest, eyes downcast on paper & tobacco.
One by one I checked out love companions, none whose beauty
stayed my heart, this place was tired of my adoration,
they knew my eyes too well. No one I could find to give me
bed tonite and wake me grinning naked, with eggs scrambled
for breakfast ready, oatmeal, grits, or hot spicy sausages
at noon assembly when I opened my eyelids out of dream. I
wandered, walking room to room thru psychedelic buses
wanting to meet someone new, younger than this crowd of wily
wrinkled wanderers with their booze and families, Electronic
Arts & Crafts, woe lined brows of chemical genius music
producers, adventurous politicians, singing ladies & earthy paramours
playing rare parts in the final movie of a generation.

The cameras
rolled and followed me, was I the central figure in this film?
I'd known most faces and guided the inevitable cameras room to room,
pausing at candle lit bus windows to view this ghostly caravan of gypsy
intellects passing thru USA, aged rock stars whispering by coal stoves,
public headline artists known from Rolling Stone & N.Y. Times,
actors & actresses from Living Theater, gaunt-faced and eloquent
with lifted hands & bony fingers greeting me on my way
to the bus driver's wheel, tattered dirty gloves on Neal's seat
waiting his return from working the National Railroad, young kids
I'd taught saluting me wearily from worn couches as I passed
bus to bus, cameras moving behind me. What was my role?
I hardly knew these faded heroes, friendly strangers
so long on the road, I'd been out teaching in Boulder, Manhattan,
Budapest, London, Brooklyn so long, why follow me thru
these amazing Further bus party reunion corridors tonite?
or is this movie, or real, if I turn to face the camera I'd break
the scene, dissolve the plot illusion, or is't illusion
art, or just my life? Were cameras ever there, the picture
flowed so evenly before my eyes, how could a crew follow
me invisible still and smoothly noiseless bus to bus
from room to room along the caravan's painted labyrinth?
This wasn't cinema, and I no hero spokesman documenting friendship
scenes, only myself alone lost in bus cabins with familiar
strangers still looking for some sexual angel for mortal delights
no different from haunting St. Mark's Boys Bar again solitary
in tie jacket and grey beard, wallet in my pocket full of
cash and cards, useless.
                              A glimmer of lights
in the curtained doorway before me! my heart leapt
forward to the Orgy Room, all youths! Lithe and
hairless, smooth skinned, white buttocks ankles, young men's
nippled chests lit behind the curtain, thighs entwined
in the male area, place I was looking for behind
my closed eyelids all this night — I pushed my hand
into the room, moving aside the curtain that shimmered
within bright with naked knees and shoulders pale

in candlelight—entered the pleasure chamber's empty door
glimmering silver shadows reflected on the silver curtained veil,
eyelids still dazzling as their adolescent limbs
intangible dissolved where I put my hand into a vacant room,
lay down on its dark floor to watch the lights of phantom arms
pulsing across closed eyelids conscious as I woke in bed
returned at dawn New York wood-slatted venetian blinds over
the windows on E. 12th St. in my white painted room

April 30, 1987, 4:30–6:25 A.M.

When the Light Appears

Lento

You'll bare your bones you'll grow you'll pray you'll only know
When the light appears, boy, when the light appears
You'll sing & you'll love you'll praise blue heavens above
When the light appears, boy, when the light appears
You'll whimper & you'll cry you'll get yourself sick and sigh
You'll sleep & you'll dream you'll only know what you mean
When the light appears, boy, when the light appears
You'll come & you'll go, you'll wander to and fro
You'll go home in despair you'll wonder why'd you care
You'll stammer & you'll lie you'll ask everybody why
You'll cough and you'll pout you'll kick your toe with gout
You'll jump you'll shout you'll knock your friends about
You'll bawl and you'll deny & announce your eyes are dry
You'll roll and you'll rock you'll show your big hard cock
You'll love & you'll grieve & one day you'll come believe
As you whistle & you smile the lord made you worthwhile
You'll preach and you'll glide on the pulpit in your pride
Sneak & slide across the stage like a river in high tide
You'll come fast or come on slow just the same you'll never know
When the light appears, boy, when the light appears

May 3, 1987, 2:30 A.M.

On Cremation of
Chögyam Trungpa, Vidyadhara

I noticed the grass, I noticed the hills, I noticed the highways,

I noticed the dirt road, I noticed car rows in the parking lot

I noticed ticket takers, I noticed the cash and checks & credit cards,

I noticed buses, noticed mourners, I noticed their children in red
dresses,

I noticed the entrance sign, noticed retreat houses, noticed blue &
yellow Flags—

noticed the devotees, their trucks & buses, guards in Khaki uniforms

I noticed crowds, noticed misty skies, noticed the all-pervading smiles &
empty eyes—

I noticed pillows, colored red & yellow, square pillows and round—

I noticed the Tori Gate, passers-through bowing, a parade of men &
women in formal dress—

noticed the procession, noticed the bagpipe, drum, horns, noticed high
silk head crowns & saffron robes, noticed the three piece suits,

I noticed the palanquin, an umbrella, the stupa painted with jewels the
colors of the four directions—

amber for generosity, green for karmic works, noticed the white for
Buddha, red for the heart—

thirteen worlds on the stupa hat, noticed the bell handle and umbrella,
the empty head of the white clay bell—

noticed the corpse to be set in the head of the bell—

noticed the monks chanting, horn plaint in our ears, smoke rising from
atop the firebrick empty bell—

noticed the crowds quiet, noticed the Chilean poet, noticed a Rainbow,

I noticed the Guru was dead, I noticed his teacher bare breasted watching the corpse burn in the stupa,

noticed mourning students sat crosslegged before their books, chanting
devotional mantras,

gesturing mysterious fingers, bells & brass thunderbolts in their hands

I noticed flame rising above flags & wires & umbrellas & painted orange
poles

I noticed the sky, noticed the sun, a rainbow round the sun, light misty
     clouds drifting over the Sun—
I noticed my own heart beating, breath passing thru my nostrils
my feet walking, eyes seeing, noticing smoke above the corpse-fir'd
     monument
I noticed the path downhill, noticed the crowd moving toward buses
I noticed food, lettuce salad, I noticed the Teacher was absent,
I noticed my friends, noticed our car the blue Volvo, a young boy held
     my hand
our key in the motel door, noticed a dark room, noticed a dream
and forgot, noticed oranges lemons & caviar at breakfast,
I noticed the highway, sleepiness, homework thoughts, the boy's nippled
     chest in the breeze
as the car rolled down hillsides past green woods to the water,
I noticed the houses, balconies overlooking a misted horizon, shore &
     old worn rocks in the sand
I noticed the sea, I noticed the music, I wanted to dance.

May 28, 1987, 2:30–3:15 A.M.

Nanao

Brain washed by numerous mountain streams
Legs clean after walking four continents
Eyes cloudless as Kagoshima sky
Fresh raw surprisingly cooked heart
Tongue live as a Spring salmon
Nanao's hands are steady, pen & ax sharp as stars.

With Peter Orlovsky
June 1987

Personals Ad

"I will send a picture too
if you will send me one of you"
—R. CREELEY

Poet professor in autumn years
seeks helpmate companion protector friend
young lover w/empty compassionate soul
exuberant spirit, straightforward handsome
athletic physique & boundless mind, courageous
warrior who may also like women & girls, no problem,
to share bed meditation apartment Lower East Side,
help inspire mankind conquer world anger & guilt,
empowered by Whitman Blake Rimbaud Ma Rainey & Vivaldi,
familiar respecting Art's primordial majesty, priapic carefree
playful harmless slave or master, mortally tender passing swift time,
photographer, musician, painter, poet, yuppie or scholar—
Find me here in New York alone with the Alone
going to lady psychiatrist who says Make time in your life
for someone you can call darling, honey, who holds you dear
can get excited & lay his head on your heart in peace.

October 8, 1987

Proclamation

For Carlos Edmondo de Ory

I am the King of the Universe
I am the Messiah with a new dispensation
Excuse me I stepped on a nail.
A mistake
Perhaps I am not the Capitalist of Heaven.
Perhaps I'm a gate keeper snoring
       beside the Pearl Columns—
No this isn't true, I really am God himself.
Not at all human. Don't associate me
       w/that Crowd.
In any case you can believe every word
       I say.

October 31, 1987
Gas Station, N.Y.

To Jacob Rabinowitz

Dear Jacob I received your translation, what kind
favor you paid to have it printed up,
lighthearted the most readable I know—
Glad to be your friend, 2000 years after Catullus,
nothing's changed poets or poetics, lovers or love
familiar conversation between the three of us,
familiar tears—Remember you leaped in bed naked
and wouldn't sleep on my floor, decade ago? I was
half century old, you hardly out of puberty gave me
your ass bright eyes and virgin body a whole month
What a little liar you were, how'd I know you were cherry?
Put me down now for not hearing your teenage heartbeat,
think back were you serious offering to kidnap me
to Philadelphia, Cleveland, Baltimore, Miami, God
knows, rescued from boring fame & Academic fortune,
Rimbaud Verlaine lovers starved together in boondock houseflat
stockyard furnished rooms eating pea soup reading E. A. Poe?
First night in each other's arms you chilled my spine whispering
lies till dawn—pubescent lovelife with a tiny monkey you claim'd
you'd tortured to death—how trust you take me to the moon?
Tho you gave your butt to others in St. Mark's Baths' steam room
that year I followed you to Chelsea Hotel kissing your boots
& still lust for your body tho now you've grown a red beard.
At thirty still cute, lost interest in my potbelly years ago,
useless to jack off to your youthful shadow anymore.
And I your genius poet first love ignored hypoglycemic,
impotent, gouty, squint-eyed, halfway bald—
Reading this book gives me youth back again, not old
in vain, at last you bring love to Catullus & Poetry
humble enough to print these translations by yourself.

December 2, 1987, 4:30 A.M.

Grandma Earth's Song

I started down Capitol Hill side along unfamiliar black central avenues
warily uncertain which streets thru Fillmore district to City Hall valley
      center,
and as I passed a block or two I saw a fragile crone marching toward me
up hill, Grandma Bag-lady ragged dressed with firm ancient steps Old
      Ma Earth
dragging a shopping cart filled with cans bottles & plastic newspapers
      tied
with silk stockings wandering alone singing out loud on way to Civic
      Center

> When dull roots write Laws
> Jerusalem to New York
> Poor Jews break Arab Jaws
> Blacks eat greasy pork

> What's the Planet News?
> Wall Street's poison pill
> Palestinians stone Jews
> Water runs downhill

> Young soldiers gonna die
> Old presidents get AIDS
> They bankrupted the sky
> The ozone layer fades

> Crazy people got money
> I own State Capitols
> Sheriff calls me honey
> The army's a bunch of fools

I want my welfare stamps
I want my movie show
I got ten kerosene lamps
I'm 99 years old

This town's already dead
This country's on the skids
This state's made out of lead
I can't feed my kids

My name is Gaia ah ha ha
Put me in jail I screw the sky
Nothing to win or lose Poppa
Born your gonna die

Adam bombs & newsboy hoaxes
Fakers yak the Oval Room
I live in cardboard boxes
They killed the ocean's womb

Tear up your welfare check
I'll eat my way to Heaven
Throw me in Walnut Creek
I'll vomit Pacific Ocean

Wakening as she passed by I thought, she's improvising street doggerel
epic popular song cackling in everyone's Immortal brain
Anything comes to mind's the right politics to ruin Police State.

February 13, 1988, 7:30–9:00 A.M.

Grandma Earth's Song

Salutations to Fernando Pessoa

Every time I read Pessoa I think
I'm better than he is I do the same thing
more extravagantly—he's only from Portugal,
I'm American greatest Country in the world
right now End of XX Century tho Portugal
had a big empire in the 15th century never mind
now shrunk to a Corner of Iberian peninsula
whereas New York take New York for instance
tho Mexico City's bigger N.Y.'s richer think of Empire State
Building not long ago world empire's biggest skyscraper—
be that as't may I've experienced 61 years' XX Century
Pessoa walked down Rua do Ouro only till 1936
He entered Whitman so I enter Pessoa no
matter what they say besides dead he wouldn't object.

What way'm I better than Pessoa?
Known on 4 Continents I have 25 English books he only 3
his mostly Portuguese, but that's not his fault—
U.S.A.'s a bigger country
merely 2 Trillion in debt a passing freakout,
Reagan's dirty work an American Century aberration
unrepresenting our Nation Whitman sang in Epic manner
tho worried about in *Democratic Vistas*
As a Buddhist not proud my superiority to Pessoa
I'm humble Pessoa was nuts big difference,
tho apparently gay—same as Socrates,
consider Michelangelo da Vinci Shakespeare
inestimable comerado Walt
True I was tainted Pinko at an early age a mere trifle
science itself destroys ozone layers this era antiStalinists
poison entire earth with radioactive anticommunism.
Maybe I lied somewhat
rarely in verse, only protecting others' reputations.

Frankly too Candid about my mother tho meant well
Did Pessoa mention his mother? she's interesting,
powerful to birth sextuplets
Alberto Cairo Alvaro de Campos Ricardo Reis Bernardo Soares &
      Alexander Search simultaneously
with Fernando Pessoa himself a classic sexophrenic
Confusing personae not so popular
outside Portugal's tiny kingdom (till recently a second-rate police state)
Let me get to the point er I forget what it was
but certainly enjoy making comparisons between this Ginsberg &
      Pessoa
people talk about in Iberia hardly any books in English
presently the world's major diplomatic language extended throughout
      China.
Besides he was a shrimp, himself admits in interminable "Salutations to
      Walt Whitman"
whereas 5′7½″ height
somewhat above world average, no immodesty,
I'm speaking seriously about me & Pessoa.
Anyway he never influenced me, never read Pessoa
before I wrote my celebrated *Howl* already translated into 24 languages,
not to this day's Pessoa influence an anxiety
Midnight April 12 '88 merely glancing his book
certainly influences me in passing, only reasonable
but reading a page in translation hardly proves "Influence."
Turning to Pessoa, what'd he write about? Whitman
(Lisbon, the sea etc.) method peculiarly longwinded,
diarrhea mouth some people say—Pessoa Schmessoa.

April 12, 1988

May Days 1988

I

As I cross my kitchen floor the thought of Death returns,
day after day, as I wake & drink lemon juice & hot water,
brush my teeth & blow my nose, stand at toilet a yellow stream
issuing from my body, look out curtained windows, across the street
Mary Help of Christians R.C. Church, how many years
empty the garbage pail, carry black plastic bags to the sidewalk,
before I boil the last soft egg,
day after day glance my altar sitting pillow a sidelong look & sigh,
pass bookcases' Greek lyrics & volumes of Military Industrial Secrecy?
How many mornings out the window Springtime's grey clouds drift
      over a wooden owl
on the Rectory roof, pigeons flutter off the street lamp to an iron fence, I
      return to kitchen
oatmeal cooking in an iron pot, sit in a wooden chair, choose a soup-
      spoon, dreaming out the window eat my gruel
as ailanthus trees bud & grow thick green, seaweed in rainy Atlantis,
lose leaves after snowfall, sit bare-branched in January's rusty winds?
Snap photographs focus'd on the clothesline, courtyard chimneypots a
      block away?
How many years lie alone in bed and stroke my cock
or read the Times on a pillow midnite, answer telephone talk, my
      Stepmother
or Joe in Washington, wait for a knock on the door it's portly Peter
      sober hesitant
inquiring supper, rarely visiting, rueful a life gone by—you got the
      monthly rent?
armfuls of mid-morn mail arriving with despairing Secretaries—
rise and tuck my shirt in, turn the doorlock key, go down hallway stairs,
enter New York City, Christine's Polish restaurant around East 12th
      Street corner on 1st Avenue
taxi uptown to art museums or visit Dr. Brown, chest x-rays, smoking
      cough or flu

Turn on the News from Palestine, Listen to Leadbelly's tape lament,
> *Black Girl, Jim Crow, Irene*—and
Sunday Puerto Ricans climb concrete steps week after week to church.

II

Sox in the laundry, snap on the kitchen light midnite icebox
raid, sun-dried tomatoes, soft swiss cheese & ham, Pineapple juice,
low rent control $260 per mo, clear sanded gymseal'd floors, white
> walls,
Blake's *Tyger* on the bedroom bookcase, cabs rattling on dark asphalt
> below,
Silence, a solitary house, Charles Fourier on bedside table waiting
> inspection, switch light off—
Pajamas in drawer for sleep, 80 volumes behind the headboard for
> browsing—
Irving Howe's Yiddish Poetry, Atilla József, Sashibusan Das Gupta's
> *Obscure Religious Cults*, Céline, *De Vulgari Eloquentia*—
What riches for old age? What cozy naps and long nights' dreams?
> Browsing in Persepolis and Lhasa!
What more ask existence? Except time, more time, ripe time & calm
& Warless time to contemplate collapsing years, tho body teeth brain
> elbow ache,
a crooked creak at backbone bottom, dry nostrils, mottled ankle
& smart tongue, how many years to talk, snap photos, sing in theaters
improvise in classroom street church radio, far from Congress?
How many more years eyes closed 9 A.M. wake worrying
the ulcer in my cheek is't cancer? Should I have charged Burroughs'
> biographer for photos
reprinted from 40 years ago? Miles the editor's stylistic competence OK
for Lit Hist Beat Generation? Should I rise & meditate
or sleep in daylight recuperate flu? phone ringing half an hour ago
What's on the Answer Machine? Give back Advances to Harper's?
Who promised deadlines for this photo book? Wasn't I up 2 A.M.
> revising Poems?
Spontaneous verse?!? Take a plane to Greenland, visit Dublin?
PEN Club meet May 17, decision Israeli Censorship Arabic Press?

Call C—— O—— Yiddish translator poetess Zionist yenta?
Write concentration camp expert moralist Elie Wiesel, what's his word
"Arabs shd throw words not stones?"—that quote accurate from the
        Times?
Should I get up right now, crosslegged scribbling Journals
with motor roar in street downstairs, stolen autos doctor'd at the curb
or pull the covers over achy bones? How many years awake or sleepy
How many mornings to be or not to be?
How many morning Mays to come, birds chirp insistent on six-story
        roofs?
buds rise in backyard cities? Forsythia yellow by brick walls & rusty
        bedsprings near the fence?

III

How many Sundays wake and lie immobile eyes closed remembering
        Death,
7 A.M. Spring Sunlight out the window the noise a Nuyorican drunkard
        on the corner
reminds me of Peter, Naomi, my nephew Alan, am I mad myself, have
        always been so
waking in N.Y. 61st year to realize childless I am a motherless freak
like so many millions, worlds from Paterson Los Angeles to Amazon
Humans & Whales screaming in despair from Empire State Building
        top to Arctic Ocean bottom—?

May 1–3, 1988

Numbers in U.S. File Cabinet
(Death Waits to Be Executed)

100,000,000 buffalo 17th century on North American Plains

$136,000,000,000 Farm Program costs encouraged chemical overuse
    1980s decade

$4,500,000 Agriculture Department research on Natural farm methods
    1980s

300,000 National junkies

100,000 alcohol deaths yearly

385,000 tobacco deaths heart attack cancer a year

30,000 deaths "illicit substances" yearly

$11,000,000,000 budget war on drugs 1990

1,000,000,000 people on world malnourished diseased

3,600,000 estimated American Homeless

300,000 mental patients dumped on streets 1970s–1980s

300 homeless slept outdoors Tompkins Park N.Y.C. July 29, 1989

17,000 meals served St. Peter's soup kitchen Morristown N.J.

110,000,000 man-made deaths Wars holocausts fatality camps
    XX Century

3°–8° Fahrenheit increase earth temperature next century computers
    project

Lambert 3-6606 Louis Ginsberg's phone for 20 years in Paterson N.J.

65 Decibels sound level ordinary speech

100 Decibels rock concert sound level

28,000,000 current cases hearing loss U.S.A.

6,000 workers, Rocky Flats Nuclear Weapons Plant

$300,000,000 yearly pay & benefits Rocky Flats Colorado

1% Colorado manufacturing activity's at Rocky Flats Nuclear Facility

70 FBI agents raided Rocky Flats investigating 10,000 gallon toxic waste
    tanks 1989

$100,000,000,000 to 200,000,000,000 estimate nuclear weapons
    complex cleanup costs

Savings & Loan Association bankruptcy taxpayers' costs it says here
    $500,000,000,000

70,000 Salvadorians killed in Civil War majority by Government
Paramilitary Death Squads funded by U.S.A.

40,000 names Doris Lessing too on National Automated Immigration
Lookout System barred entering U.S.A.

3,000 citizens killed by Shining Path, Peru 1972–1979

3,000 citizens disappeared in Government custody Peru 1972–1979

U.S. produces 24% planetary Greenhouse gas, consumes 40% world's
gasoline

$2,000,000,000,000-plus U.S. National debt 1990 ante Iraq War

$65 cost of Harry Smith's eyeglasses

20 largest World Cities by year 2000 none U.S.-European none speak
English

1 in 10 Salvadorians displaced in decade's counterinsurgency war

1 sun per known solar system

1 set Wisdom teeth

1 mother of all

1 wrong move

1 bad apple

1 way street

1 anus each

1 non-God

1 down 2 to go

March 1990

Return of Kral Majales

This silver anniversary much hair's gone from my head and I am the
    King of May
And tho I am King of May my howls & proclamations present are
    banned by FCC on America's electric airwaves 6 A.M. to mid-
    night
So King of May I return through Heaven flying to reclaim my paper
    crown
And I am King of May with high blood pressure, diabetes, gout, Bell's
    palsy, kidneystones & calm eyeglasses
And wear the foolish crown of no ignorance no wisdom anymore no fear
    no hope in capitalist striped tie & Communist dungarees
No laughing matter the loss of the planet next hundred years
And I am the King of May returned with a diamond big as the universe
    an empty mind
And I am the King of May lacklove bouzerant in Springtime with a
    feeble practice of meditation
And I am King of May Distinguished Brooklyn English Professor
    singing
All gone all gone all overgone all gone sky-high now old mind so Ah!

April 25, 1990

Elephant in the Meditation Hall

Yes all spiritual groups scandal the shrine room
What about San Francisco Roshi & the board director's wife
What about high living limousine expense accounts in Moscow?
What about the late Rajneesh & poisoned gefilte fish in Oregon?
What's hiding under Rajneeshis' Orange skullcaps? Brains?
Then old L.A. Mountain Roshi even tap'd his young girls
and East Coast Roshi's semen dribbled from Hawaii to the broom
    closets of the Catskills
Maezumi Roshi caused grief his senseis' hearts wrung out with midnight
    sake & beer
Later he thanked them for A.A.
Veteran Zenmaster with motorcycle & community farm chorale felt up
    little boys
& a big guy too, tough as nails
Remember a strange Mongolian Russian fruitcake Lama in Polk Gulch
    Bay Area?
Vajracharya Trungpa! Dont mention the naked poet at the Halloween
    Party!
And the whispered transmission regent died of AIDS (disciple a straight
    guy sick they say)
Marxists were right, religion the people's opium!
But who're *they* to talk lookit Mao a Marxist his picture on every
    Chinese wall & Little Red Book
wherefore everyone stood up bedtime nites reciting his dread slogans?
They still had pictures of Stalin on truckcab windows in Gori 1985 a
    scandal!
And New Left carried psychedelic pictures of Mao, Che Guevara &
    Castro up and down Empire State's stairways
A scandal of the sixties! And marvelous atheist Khmer Rouge read Marx
    Sartre & Erich Fromm,
how many'd they murder with religious good intentions?
What US President hasn't sponsored war, Lumumba's assassination, an
    H-bomb,

trillion dollar Savings & Loan mistakes? Scandals! taxpayers gotta subsi-
    dize Banks!
Now we gotta digest Plutonium? how evacuate CIA?
Scandal hundreds homeless under Brooklyn Bridge freezing Xmas &
    New Year's Eve! Millions homeless in America!
Who'll gotta pay for 500,000 U.S. boys & girls visiting Arabian Deserts?
Who'll cough up billions for Iraq War to save a President's face?
Twelve Billion dollars mickeymouse the year's drug wars?
El Salvador, Honduras, Guatemala we paid death squads for decades
Nobody does anything right! Gods, Popes, Mullahs, Communists,
    Poets, Financiers!
My own life, scandal! lazy bum! secondhand royal scarlet ties & Yves St.
    Laurent Salvation Army blazers
How many boys let me caress their thighs!
How many girls cursed my cold beard? I better commit suicide!
That wouldn't work either, it'll be a beatnik scandal
after Cassady's railroad track death, Joan Burroughs' bullet in head,
Orlovsky sane in Bellevue 1st Ave., Kerouac's liver collapse & ruptured
    esophagus!
Trapped in living nightmare, I made a big mistake I got born,
The world came out of a black hole, whole universe
a scandal, illusion, everyone deluded, a cosmic elephant in the medita-
    tion planet,
George the IIIrd, Rasputin, Stalin, Warren Harding, Herbert Hoover,
    Hitler, the 13th Dalai Lama's Regent, Vice President Agnew,
Ronald Reagan delayed hostage release till the Elephant party's Inau-
    guration Day
George Bush peddled coke for the contras in streetcorner banks down-
    town Panama City!
Scandals in Buddhafields? big mistakes in Hemispheres, on moons,
    Black Holes everywhere!
Anyway, the national debt'll approach 4 trillion any day say the homeless
    on Tompkins Square.

July 12, 1990

Poem in the Form of a Snake
That Bites Its Tail

Oleta (Snake) River!
Heron, Manatee, Osprey
Canopy of white red &
black Mangroves
fighting for survival against
exotics introduced
by Europeans
Swamp fern covers the ground
by this Primordial Tidal
Zone,
Brown detritus under the
clear water
feeds animals and trees in
high and low tides
pulled by the moon,
cycles of lunar
reproduction following
waters flowing
in and out the
Intracoastal Waterway—
Barracuda come
in with the tides
Heron we'll see
Brazilian pepper
& Malalluca
from Australia
brought in by Mr. Gifford
first Doctor
of Tropical Agriculture

Malalluca
    to dry out the swamps
        & make truck farms
        to feed the Northeast 1900—
           Dade County
        tomatoes & cabbage today—

Then real estate won
    out, that saved the
        swamp
        water
        supply
This forest by Oleta River a tiny
    area untouched
        half a million
           years—
  Interconnected to the
    coral reefs
  (as nutrient-rich protective
    soup for fish
        spawning)
      with a rubber tire, mucus—
        soaked in the ooze
  Red mangrove
    seedlings growing on inland skirts
      at water edge
   roots like spindly
    buttresses

First Indians Tequesta
    for 10–25,000 years—
      left behind shell
        tools
    to make dugouts

Mikasuki and Seminole
were Creek Indians forced down
                from North Carolina
        by Sen. Jesse Helms
        then driven inland from
        Northern Florida
                        by the Army
                —Indian middens
        attest 100
        years' occupation

The Seminole
more warlike than
        the innocent
                Tequestas

Quiet in a canoe
        Train whistle West
        & airplane above
                cottony clouds
                        in blue afternoon

Seminole and Mikasuki
        accepted
        runaway slaves
                got in trouble with
                the whites—
Abraham the Runaway showed Chief Osceola
                guerrilla gunpowder—
                        Defied the U.S. Army—
Govt. fought 2 wars
                against them—
        first 1820 Andrew Jackson
                fought in Florida
        pushed Indians south

Second Seminole War
       transported 2,000
              Indians to Oklahoma
                     around 1840, the Trail of Tears
—200 managed to
escape into swamp
where white man had
       yet no use for
              the land
Indians
       from before Columbus
                            & runaway slaves
              Strange & perpetual
                     alliance

Otherwise we're all exotics
       like the Brazilian pepper
              and Australian pine

A brown heron
       flaps along the
                     green surface
       to stand sentinel
                     beak pointed out
   on a green lawn
                     past the big rubber
                            tree—
       tall stalky legs
              rising halfway
heavy slow
       on long wings
       the height of the big
       ficus' leafy
                     umbrella whose
              thready prop roots hang
       over the concrete
       bank down to the brackish
                     water surface

Kids' & crows' voices
        (crows here for the
                season)

Water filled the
        coral, ojus,

                limestone
        a product trucked
                out since
                        the railroad came down,
                        turn of the century

Trains a mile long
                from rockpits now
        at the edge of
                        the Everglades

Mikasuki Indians now hold
                cultural events
                Steve & Billy Tiger
                        painter & musician

Seminoles more commercially
                oriented, invented Bingo on
                        the reservation,
                On land they control
                untax'd cigarettes

A local issue
                        ecological!
We depend on Everglades
        for water to
                        sustain our days—

Most of the body is
made up of water—
3–4 days without water
we die—
Everglades filters the
    water Dade Broward
    & Palm Beach County
        drink—
    (Tricounty fresh
      water—)

But Brazilian pepper seeds
    explode
    and cause mumbo-jumbo
    growth at
        waterside.

Exotic Malalluca trees—?
The developers like it
    (it's cheap)
  but they drink up water & their
  flowers cause allergies
  to Rochelle—

Red mangrove
        stains the water
    properly its own color

Are hyperindustrial White folks
    exotics to the planet now?

Here comes a duck
that flies, sings & runs
    but doesn't do any
      of them well

El pato vuela, canta
        y corre, pero
    ninguno de las tres
            los hace bien.

Big yellow hibiscus faces
        with red noses—
Venetian sailors
        brought
            venereal disease
            to New World
now Millennial events
            speed up?

Get off fossil fuels
        for transport
Get off oil addiction
Plastics could be
        recyclable

Zero Growth regenerative
        recycling as for
            thousands of years
            with the Tequesta
Get off this disposable
        binge—

& water! dont mess
        up the Oleta River Dont
    play with the big Snake

Can live without air
        8 minutes
Can live without water
            2–4 days
can live without food
        40–50 days—

Survive, clean up our
                air
Clean up water
Grow enuf food to
        keep everybody
                alive

Instructors: any
                indigenous populations

Indians, Africans,
        Tibetans, Bedouins
                Laplanders—
Chernobyl began
        the question—
How much can the
        Government lie?

(*Miami Herald* pervasive
        and controlling—)

Locally the Seminoles may
        be the Gurus.

With Steven Bornstein
November 16, 1990

Mistaken Introductions

or this marvelous hi Lama followed
       in here by screaming madwoman
       charging she was betrayed 10 years ago
       on one of the moons of Saturn
or, I want to introduce you to this
       universe which unfortunately
       doesn't quite exist.
We set up luncheon at Rizzoli
       for the Tibetan photog who
       hadnt prepared his
       slides, it was a disaster—
May I introduce you to your
       prospective son-in-law—
       unfortunately today he's drunk
          unshaven but a good
       businessman tomorrow
It's a magnificent hotel
       just this week there's no
       water to flush the toilet
       above the 10th floor
       where you're staying and
we had a fire in the elevator

January 7, 1991

C.I.A. DOPE CALYPSO

In nine-teen hun-dred forty – nine China was won by
Mao Tse - Tung Chiang Kai-Shek's ar-my ran a-way They were
wait-ing there in Thailand yester-day Sup- por-ted by the
C I A Pushing junk down Thailand way

First They stole from the Meo tribes Up in the hills they
started taking bribes Then they sent their Sol-diers up to Shan Col-
-lecting o-pi-um to sell to the Man
Pushing junk in Bang-kok yester-day Sup-ported by the
C I A

CIA Dope Calypso

In nineteen hundred forty-nine
China was won by Mao Tse-tung
Chiang Kai-shek's army ran away
They were waiting there in Thailand yesterday

Supported by the CIA
Pushing junk down Thailand way

First they stole from the Meo tribes
Up in the hills they started taking bribes
Then they sent their soldiers up to Shan
Collecting opium to sell to The Man

Pushing junk in Bangkok yesterday
Supported by the CIA

Brought their jam on mule trains down
To Chiang Rai that's a railroad town
Sold it next to police chief brain
He took it to town on the choochoo train

Trafficking dope to Bangkok all day
Supported by the CIA

The policeman's name was Mr. Phao
He peddled dope grand scale and how
Chief of border customs paid
By Central Intelligence's U.S. A.I.D.

The whole operation, Newspapers say
Supported by the CIA

He got so sloppy & peddled so loose
He busted himself & cooked his own goose
Took the reward for an opium load
Seizing his own haul which same he resold

Big-time pusher a decade turned grey
Working for the CIA

Touby Lyfong he worked for the French
A big fat man liked to dine & wench
Prince of the Meos he grew black mud
Till opium flowed through the land like a flood

Communists came and chased the French away
So Touby took a job with the CIA

The whole operation fell into chaos
Till U.S. Intelligence came into Laos
I'll tell you no lie I'm a true American
Our big pusher there was Phoumi Nosovan

All them princes in a power play
But Phoumi was the man for the CIA

And his best friend General Vang Pao
Ran our Meo army like a sacred cow
Helicopter smugglers filled Long Cheng's bars
In Xieng Quang province on the Plain of Jars

It started in secret they were fighting yesterday
Clandestine secret army of the CIA

All through the Sixties the Dope flew free
Thru Tan Son Nhut Saigon to Marshal Ky
Air America followed through
Transporting confiture for President Thieu

All these Dealers were decades and yesterday
The Indochinese mob of the U.S. CIA

Operation Haylift offisir Wm. Colby
Saw Marshal Ky fly opium Mr. Mustard told me
Indochina desk he was Chief of Dirty Tricks
"Hitchhiking" with dope pushers was how he got his fix

Subsidizing traffickers to drive the Reds away
Till Colby was the head of the CIA

January 1972

N.S.A. Dope Calypso

Now Richard Secord and Oliver North
Hated Sandinistas whatever they were worth
They peddled for the Contras to ease their pain
They couldn't sell Congress so Contras sold cocaine

They discovered Noriega only yesterday
Nancy Reagan & the CIA

Now coke and grass were exchanged for guns
On a border airfield that John Hull runs
Or used to run till his Costa Rican bust
As a CIA spy trading Contra coke dust

They discovered Noriega only yesterday
Nancy Reagan & the CIA

Ramón Milian Rodríguez of Medellín Cartel
Laundered their dollars & he did it very well
Hundreds of millions through U.S. banks
Till he got busted and sang in the tank

It was buried in the papers only yesterday
When Bush was Drug Czar U.S.A.

Milian told Congress $3,000,000 coke bucks
Went to Felix Rodríguez, CIA muck-a-muck
To give to the Contras only Hush Hush Hush
Except for Donald Gregg & his boss George Bush

Buried in the papers only yesterday
With Bush Vice President U.S.A.

Rodríguez met Bush in his office many times
They didn't talk business, they drank lemon & limes
Or maybe they drank coffee or they smoked a cigarette
But cocaine traffic they remembered to forget

It was buried in the papers only yesterday
And Bush got in the White House of the U.S.A.

Now when Bush was director of the C.I.A.
Panama traffic in coke was gay
You never used to hear George Bush holler
When Noriega laundered lots of cocaine dollar

Bush paid Noriega, used to work together
They sat on a couch & talked about the weather

Then Noriega doublecrossed his Company pal
With a treaty taking back our Panama Canal
So when he got into the big White House
Bush said Noriega was a cocaine louse

The Cold War ended, East Europe found hope
The U.S. got hooked in a war on dope

Glasnost came, East Europe got free
So Bush sent his army to Panama City
Bush's guns in Panama did their worst
Like coke fiends fighting on St. Marks & First

Does Noriega know Bush's Company crimes?
In 2000 A.D. read the New York Times.

January–February 1990

III
Just Say Yes Calypso

When Schwarzkopf's Father busted Iran's Mossadegh
They put in the Shah and his police the Savak
They sucked up his oil, but got Ayatollah's dreck
So Thirty years later we hadda arm Iraq

Though he used poison gas, Saddam was still our man
But to aid the Contras, hadda also arm Iran

Mesopotamia was doing just fine
Till the Ottoman Empire blew up on a mine
They had apple orchards in Eden and Ur
Till the Snake advised George Bush "This land is yours"

The Garden foul'd up, brimstone came down
In the good old days we had plenty ozone

The British & Americans & Frenchmen all
Took concessions in the Garden So the Garden took a fall
Got addicted to Emirs and their fossil fuels
Police state Sheiks & Intelligence ghouls

The Sphinx lost his nose, acid ate the Parthenon
Pretty soon the Persian Gulf is dead and gone

The Saudi desert bloomed with oil pipe lines
To push the auto industry It's yours & it's mine
L.A. and Osaka got a habit on gas
In a bullet-proof Caddie you can really move your ass

L.A. & Osaka got a habit on gas
In a bullet-proof Caddie you can really move your ass

From a Mickey-Mouse war on cocaine & crack
We dropped a million bombs on the kids in Iraq
How many we killed nobody wants to tell
It'd give a lousy picture of a war they gotta sell

When they wave a yellow ribbon & an oily flag
Just say yes or they'll call you a fag

April 25, 1991

Hum Bom!

I

Whom bomb?
We bomb'd them!
Whom bomb?
We bomb'd them!
Whom bomb?
We bomb'd them!
Whom bomb?
We bomb'd them!

Whom bomb?
We bomb you!
Whom bomb?
We bomb you!
Whom bomb?
You bomb you!
Whom bomb?
You bomb you!

What do we do?
Who do we bomb?
What do we do?
Who do we bomb?
What do we do?
Who do we bomb?
What do we do!
Who do we bomb?

What do we do?
You bomb! You bomb them!
What do we do?
You bomb! You bomb them!
What do we do?
We bomb! We bomb you!
What do we do?
You bomb! You bomb you!

Whom bomb?
We bomb you!
Whom bomb?
We bomb you!
Whom bomb?
You bomb you!
Whom bomb?
You bomb you!

May 1971

II

For Don Cherry

Whydja bomb?
We didn't wanna bomb!
Whydja bomb?
We didn't wanna bomb!
Whydja bomb?
You didn't wanna bomb!
Whydja bomb?
You didn't wanna bomb!

Who said bomb?
Who said we hadda bomb?
Who said bomb?
Who said we hadda bomb?
Who said bomb?
Who said you hadda bomb?
Who said bomb?
Who said you hadda bomb?

Who wantsa bomb?
We don't wanna bomb!
Who wantsa bomb?
We don't wanna bomb!
Who wantsa bomb?
We don't wanna bomb!
We don't wanna
        we don't wanna
            we don't wanna bomb!

Who wanteda bomb?
Somebody musta wanteda bomb!
Who wanteda bomb?
Somebody musta wanteda bomb!
Who wanteda bomb?
Somebody musta wanteda bomb!
Who wanteda bomb?
Somebody musta wanteda bomb!

They wanteda bomb!
They neededa bomb!
They wanteda bomb!
They neededa bomb!
They wanteda bomb!
They neededa bomb!
They wanteda bomb!
They neededa bomb!

They thought they hadda bomb!
They thought they hadda bomb!
They thought they hadda bomb!
They thought they hadda bomb!

Saddam said he hadda bomb!
Bush said he better bomb!
Saddam said he hadda bomb!
Bush said he better bomb!
Saddam said he hadda bomb!
Bush said he better bomb!
Saddam said he hadda bomb!
Bush said he better bomb!

Whatdid he say he better bomb for?
Whatdid he say he better bomb for?
Whatdid he say he better bomb for?
Whatdid he say he better bomb for?

Hadda get ridda Saddam with a bomb!
Hadda get ridda Saddam with a bomb!
Hadda get ridda Saddam with a bomb!
Hadda get ridda Saddam with a bomb!

Saddam's still there building a bomb!
Saddam's still there building a bomb!
Saddam's still there building a bomb!
Saddam's still there building a bomb!

III
Armageddon did the job
Gog & Magog Gog & Magog
Armageddon did the job
Gog & Magog Gog & Magog

Gog & Magog Gog & Magog
Armageddon does the job
Gog & Magog Gog & Magog
Armageddon does the job

Armageddon for the mob
Gog & Magog Gog & Magog
Armageddon for the mob
Gog & Magog Gog & Magog

Gog & Magog Gog & Magog
Gog Magog Gog Magog
Gog & Magog Gog & Magog
Gog Magog Gog Magog

Gog Magog Gog Magog
Gog Magog Gog Magog
Gog Magog Gog Magog
Gog Magog Gog Magog

Ginsberg says Gog & Magog
Armageddon did the job.

February–June 1991

Supplication for the Rebirth of the Vidyadhara Chögyam Trungpa, Rinpoche

Dear Lord Guru who pervades the space of my mind
permeates the universe of my consciousness,
still empties my balding head and's stabilized my wand'ring thought
to average equanimity in Manhattan & Boulder

Return return reborn in spirit & knowledge in human body
my own or others as continual Teacher of chaotic peace,
Return according to your vow to pacify magnetize enrich destroy
grasping angry stupidity in me my family friends & Sangha

Return in body speech & mind to enlighten my labors
& the labors of your meditators, thousands from L.A. to Halifax
to relieve sufferings of our brothers, lovers
family, friends, fellow citizens, nations and planet.

Remember your vow to be with us on our deathbeds
in living worlds where we dwell in your tender perspective
breathe with your conscious breath, catch ourselves thinking
& dissolve bomb dream, fear of our own skin & yelling argument
                                        in the sky of your mind

Bend your efforts to regroup our community within your thought-body
& mind-space, the effects of your non-thought,
Turbulent ease of your spontaneous word & picture
nonmeditative compassion your original mind

These slogans were writ on the second day of June 1991
a sleepless night my brother's 70th birthday on Long Island
my own sixty-fifth year in the human realm visiting his house
by the Vajra Poet Allen Ginsberg supplicating protection of his
                                        Vajra Guru Chögyam Trungpa

                                        June 2, 1991, 2:05 A.M.

After the Big Parade

Millions of people cheering and waving flags for joy in Manhattan
Yesterday've returned to their jobs and arthritis now Tuesday—
What made them want so much passion at last, such mutual delight—
Will they ever regain these hours of confetti'd ecstasy again?
Have they forgotten the Corridors of Death that gave such victory?
Will another hundred thousand desert deaths across the world be
                          cause for the next rejoicing?

June 11, 1991, 2:30 P.M.

Big Eats

Big deal bargains TV meat stock market news paper headlines love life
       Metropolis
Float thru air like thought forms float thru the skull, check the headlines
       catch the boyish ass that walks
Before you fall in bed blood sugar high blood pressure lower, lower,
       your lips grow cold.
Sooner or later let go what you loved hated or shrugged off, you walk in
       the park
You look at the sky, sit on a pillow, count up the stars in your head, get up
       and eat.

August 20, 1991

Not Dead Yet

Huffing puffing upstairs downstairs telephone
        office mail checks secretary revolt—
The Soviet Legislative Communist bloc
        inspired Gorbachev's wife and Yeltsin
to shut up in terror or stand on a tank
        in front of White House denouncing Putschists—
September breezes sway branches & leaves in
        a calm schoolyard under humid grey sky,
Drink your decaf Ginsberg old communist New
        York Times addict, be glad you're not Trotsky.

September 16, 1991

Yiddishe Kopf

I'm Jewish because love my family matzoh ball soup.

I'm Jewish because my fathers mothers uncles grandmothers said "Jewish," all the way back to Vitebsk & Kaminetz-Podolska via Lvov.

Jewish because reading Dostoyevsky at 13 I write poems at restaurant
tables Lower East Side, perfect delicatessen intellectual.

Jewish because violent Zionists make my blood boil, Progressive indig-
nation.

Jewish because Buddhist, my anger's transparent hot air, I shrug my
shoulders.

Jewish because monotheist Jews Catholics Moslems're intolerable
intolerant—

Blake sd. "6000 years of sleep" since antique Nobodaddy Adonai's mind
trap—Oy! such Meshuggeneh absolutes—

Senior Citizen Jewish paid my dues got half-fare card buses subways,
discount movies—

Can't imagine how these young people make a life, make a living.

How can they stand it, going out in the world with only $10 and a
hydrogen bomb?

October 1991

John

I

No one liked my hair
Mother pulled it toward the movies
Father hit the top of my head
Street gangs set it afire
My dry hair, my
short hair, black hair, drab hair
my stupid hair—frizzled!
Till I met John,
John loved my hair
Twined his fingers in my delicate curly locks
Told me let it grow
John buried his face in my hair
kissed my hair
Murmured endearments "Oh oh oh" to the top of my skull
Patted me on the head
Stroked me from crown to neck nape—
Sat across from me on the subway and gazed at me lovingly—

II

They were whispering, elbows leaned on the wide marble balustrade
balcony lobby of the Majestic Theater—
talking Jerusalem, Moscow, Ballet, Quasars, Interest rates—
John came down from his seat, stopped at the top stair—
sat down, hands on his ears in despair—"I've stymied my feet!"
"What" they asked, "you've stymied your feet? Whazzat mean?"
John nodded his head, eyes closed, hands against his head as before,
"I've stymied my feet," he repeated dolefully.

III

John had AIDS.
First, he began talking to himself.
The psychiatrist said:
"If you're going to talk to yourself,
        do it in the form of poetry."

November 7, 1991, 8:30 A.M.

A Thief Stole This Poem

These days steal everything
People steal your wallet, your watch
Break into your car steal your radio suitcase
Break in your house, your Sony Hi 8 your CD VCR Olympus XA
People steal your life, catch you on the street & steal your head off
Steal your sneakers in the toilet
Steal your love, mug your boyfriend rape your grandmother on the
        subway
Junkies steal your heart for medicine, they steal your credibility gap over
        the radio
Cokeheads & blackmen steal your comfort, peace of mind walking
        Avenue A your laundry package
steal your spirit, you gotta worry
Puerto Ricans steal white skin from your face
Wasps steal your planet for junk bonds, Jews steal your Nobodaddy and
        leave their dirty God in your bed
Arabs steal your pecker & you steal their oil
Everybody's stealing from everyone else, time sex wristwatch money
Steal your sleep 6 A.M. Garbage Trucks boomboxes sirens loud argu-
        ments hydrogen bombs
steal your universe.

December 19, 1991, 8:15 A.M.

Lunchtime

Birds chirp in the brick backyard Radio
piano chopping gentle chords next door
A rush of tires & car exhaust on 14th Street
Delighted to be alive this cloudy Thursday
February window open at the kitchen table,
Senior Citizen ready for next week's angiogram.

February 20, 1992, 1:15 P.M.

Deadline Dragon Comix
I'm late, I'm gonna die before I mark the term papers!
I've run out of STEAM--
People think
WHERE'S MY NEW POEM?
(Why don't I write another Howl?)
THREE HOURS LATE DELIVERING W.S. BURROUGHS INTERVIEW TO TOKYO
FIVE YEARS LATE DELIVERING MY 1950's JOURNALS TO HARPERS
OUCH! SIX MONTHS LATE FINISHING A COMIC STRIP
TIME OUT TO TAKE AN IMPORTANT NAP
ZZZ
ZZZZZ
GATE GATE PARAGATE PARASAMGATE BODHI SVAHA!
R.I.P.
ALLEN GINSBERG
1926–
IMMORTALITY COMES LATER
N.Y.C. 2/27/92

After Lalon

I

It's true I got caught in
                the world
When I was young Blake
              tipped me off
Other teachers followed:
Better prepare for Death
Don't get entangled with
                possessions
That was when I was young,
           I was warned
Now I'm a Senior Citizen
and stuck with a million
                books
a million thoughts a million
             dollars a million
                  loves
How'll I ever leave my body?
Allen Ginsberg says, I'm
             really up shits creek

II

I sat at the foot of a
           Lover
    and he told me everything
Fuck off, 23 skidoo,
        watch your ass,
        watch your step
exercise, meditate, think
      of your temper—

Now I'm an old man and
　　　　I won't live another
20 years maybe not another
　　　　20 weeks,
maybe the next second I'll
　　　　be carried off to
　　　　　　rebirth
　　the worm farm, maybe it's
　　　　already happened—
How should I know, says
　　　　Allen Ginsberg
Maybe I've been dreaming
　　　　all along—

III
It's 2 A.M. and I got to
　　　　get up early
and taxi 20 miles to satisfy
　　　　my ambition—
How'd I get into this fix,
this workaholic show-
　　　　biz meditation market?
If I had a soul I sold it
　　　　for pretty words
If I had a body I used
　　　　it up spurting my essence
If I had a mind it got
　　　　covered with Love—
If I had a spirit I forgot
　　　　when I was breathing
If I had speech it was
　　　　all a boast
If I had desire it went
　　　　out my anus

If I had ambitions to
            be liberated
how'd I get into this
            wrinkled person?
With pretty words, Love essences,
                breathing boasts, anal
                longings, famous crimes?
What a mess I am, Allen Ginsberg.

IV
Sleepless I stay up &
            think about my Death
—certainly it's nearer
                than when I was ten
                        years old
and wondered how big the
            universe was—
If I dont get some rest I'll die faster
If I sleep I'll lose my
            chance for salvation—
asleep or awake, Allen
    Ginsberg's in bed
        in the middle of the night.

V

4 A.M.

Then they came for me,
       I hid in the toilet stall
They broke down the toilet door
       It fell in on an innocent boy
Ach the wooden door fell
       in on an innocent kid!
I stood on the bowl & listened,
       I hid my shadow,
they shackled the other and
       dragged him away
in my place— How long can
       I get away with this?
Pretty soon they'll discover
       I'm not there
They'll come for me again, where
       can I hide my body?
Am I myself or some one else
       or nobody at all?
Then what's this heavy flesh this
       weak heart leaky kidney?
Who's been doing time
       for 65 years
in this corpse? Who else went
       into ecstasy besides me?
Now it's all over soon,
       what good was all that come?
Will it come true? Will
       it really come true?

VI

I had my chance and lost it,
many chances & didn't
    take them seriously enuf.
Oh yes I was impressed, almost
    went mad with fear
I'd lose the immortal chance,
    One lost it.
Allen Ginsberg warns you
    dont follow my path
    to extinction.

March 31, 1992

Get It?

Get beat up on TV squirming on the ground for driving irregular
Get bombed in Philadelphia by helicopters with your little babies
Get kicked in the street by Newark police and charged w/riot
Get assassinated by a jerk while FBI sleeps with itself
Get shot by a stringer for the CIA & blame it on Fair Play for Cuba
      Committee
Get bumped off by an errandboy for Cuban drug kingpins, friend of the
      Feds & Dallas cops
Get caught paying off Contras with coke money while Acting U.S. Drug
      War Czar
Get busted for overcharging Iranians on secret warplane sales
Get convicted of lying to Congress about off-the-shelf dirty wars in
      Central America
Get 12 billion dollars for a drug bureaucracy and double the number of
      addicts
Get a million people in prison in the land of the free
Get the electric chair & gas chamber for unpopular crimes
Organize *Citizens for Decency Through Law* rob your own phony bank
      several billion dollars get sent to jail

May 1992
New York

Angelic Black Holes

By Andrey Voznesensky

Soul to crotch the streets commit hara-kiri,
Burnt-out stores chessboard moonlit households,
The City of Angels stares into black holes—
See down through Earth to scorched Nagorno-Karabakh.
How long is the tunnel of pain?
Does God need Welfare?

Even so, remembering the sheen on Peredelkino's black gooseberries,
Rodney King's name sounds Russian, *rodnik* for ground-spring.
As for me who crapped up my own homeland
How lay the blame on anybody else?
Rain & ashes seal my lips.
The two superpowers left the Little Man supersufferings.
Us—blown to hell. You—immolate yourselves in flame?

Any light at the end of the tunnel of pain?

Translated by Allen Ginsberg and Nina Bouis
May 17, 1992
Los Angeles

Research

Research has shown that black people have inferiority complexes regarding white folks

Research has shown that Jews are exclusively concerned with financial lasciviousness

Research has shown Socialism to be a universal failure wherever practiced by secret police

Research has shown that Earth was created 4004 B.C., a Divine Bang

Research has shown that sparrows, bees, lizards, chickens, pigs & cows exhibit signs of homosexual behavior when in prison

Research has shown Southern Baptist Inerrancy Confession the most virulent form of Christian Truth

Research has shown that 90% of people going to Dentists have bad teeth

brush your teeth violently 3 times a day after meals wear away the roots

Research has shown that Hollywood makes the best films ever, the sexually degenerate

that the U.N. is Good □ Bad □ Indifferent □ for American interests   Check One

Research has shown that Christian Reconstructionist homosexuality is Sin, Lesbianism crime against nature, AIDS a plague sent to punish gay Angelmakers

bisexuality disapproved by 51% Americans

Research has shown that teen headshakers watching TV get more IQ tests than natives of Amazon & Ucayali rivers who have no antennae

Research has shown whales & porpoises to subscribe to a Higher Intelligence

Research has shown that Elitist Individualism Spiritual Corruption & Degenerate Art caused Dictatorships in Soviet Union China and Germany

that possession of pornography by American Family Institute has resulted in 35% increase in sex crimes among institute librarians
viewing murderous behavior on TV sitcoms resulted in 100% increased
  violent language behavior by intercontinental Heads of State
To conclude research has shown that the material universe does not
  exist

May 20, 1992

PUT DOWN YOUR CIGARETTE RAG

Dont smoke dont   dont   Dont   dont   It's a nine billion dol-lar
smoke smoke   smoke   smoke

Capital - ist   Commu-nist joke Dont   dont dont dont dont dont   Dont
smoke smoke smoke smoke smoke smoke

Smoking makes you cough You can't sing straight You gargle on sa-

-li-va & you   vomit   on your plate Dont   dont   dont   dont
smoke   smoke   smoke

smoke Dont   dont smoke   (You)   Smoke in bed You smoke on the hill Smoke
smoke

Till yr dead You smoke in Hell Dont   dont   in Li-ving Hell Dope Dope Dont
smoke smoke

smoke dont smoke dont smoke

※STANZAS 3,4,5,11,12, ARE CHANTED
ON "A" WITH SOME PITCH VARIATION.
THE REST CONFORM TO MELODY AS FOLLOWS

FIRST DOUBLE BAR

Put Down Your Cigarette Rag (Dont Smoke)

Dont smoke dont smoke dont smoke
Dont smoke
It's a nine billion dollar
Capitalist Communist joke
 Dont smoke dont smoke dont smoke dont smoke
   Dont smoke

Smoking makes you cough,
You cant sing straight
You gargle on saliva
& vomit on your plate
 Dont smoke dont smoke dont smoke dont smoke,
   Dont smoke smoke smoke smoke

You smoke in bed
You smoke on the hill
Smoke till yr dead
You smoke in Hell
 Dont smoke dont smoke in living Hell Dope Dope
   Dont smoke dont smoke dont smoke

You puff your fag
You suck your butt
You choke & gag
Teeth full of crud
 Smoke smoke smoke smoke Dont dont dont
   Dont Dont Dope Dope Dope Dont Smoke Dont Dope

Pay your two bucks
  for a deathly pack
Trust your bad luck
  & smoke in the sack
 Dont Smoke Dont Smoke Nicotine Nicotine No
 No dont smoke the official Dope Smoke Dope Dope

Four Billion dollars in Green
'swat Madison Avenue gets
t' advertise nicotine
& hook you radical brats
      Dont Smoke Dont Smoke Dont Smoke
         Nope Nope Dope Dope Hoax Hoax Hoax Hoax
      Dopey Dope Dopey Dope Dope Dope dope dope

Black magic pushes dope
Sexy chicks in cars
America loses hope
& smokes and drinks in bars
      Dont smoke dont smoke dont smoke,
      dont smoke dont dont dont dont
      choke choke choke choke kaf kaf
      Kaf Kaf Choke Choke
      Choke Choke Dope Dope

Communism's flopped
Let's help the Soviet millions
Sell 'em our Coffin-Nails
& make a couple billions
      Big Bucks Big Bucks bucks bucks
         bucks bucks smoke smoke smoke smoke
            smoke bucks smoke bucks Dope bucks big
            Dope Bucks Dig Big Dope Bucks Big Dope
         Bucks dont smoke big dope bucks
            Dig big Pig dope bucks

Nine billion bucks a year
a Southern Industry
Buys Senator Jesse Fear who pushes Tobacco subsidy
In the Senate Foreign Relations Committee
    Dope smokes dope smokes dont smoke dont smoke
        Cloak cloak cloak room cloak & dagger
      smoke room cloak room dope cloak
      cloak room dope cloak room dope dont smoke

Nine billion bucks for dope
approved by Time & Life
America loses hope
The President smokes Tobacco votes
    Dont Smoke dont smoke dont smoke dont smoke
      Dont smoke nope nope nope nope

20 thousand die of coke
    Illegal speed each year
400 thousand cigarette deaths
    That's the drug to fear
      Dont smoke Dont smoke Dont smoke

Get Hooked on Cigarettes
Go Fight the War on Drugs
Smoke any other Weed
Get bust by Government Thugs
    Dont smoke dont smoke the official dope

If you will get in bed
& give your girlfriend head
then you wont want a fag
Nor evermore a drag
    Dont Smoke dont smoke Hope Hope Hope Hope
      O Please Dont Smoke Dont Smoke
      O Please O Please O Please
      I'm calling on my knees

Twenty-four hours in bed
& give your boyfriend head
Put something in your mouth
Like skin not cigarette filth
    Suck tit suck tit suck cock suck cock
            suck clit suck prick suck it
            but dont smoke nicotine dont smoke
            dont smoke nicotine nicotine it's
            too obscene dont smoke dont smoke
            nicotine suck cock suck prick suck tit
            suck clit suck it But don't smoke shit nope
            nope nope nope Dope Dope Dope Dope
                the official dope Dont Smoke

Make believe yer sick
Stay in bed and lick
yr cigarette habit greed
One day's all you need
    In deed in deed in deed in deed smoke weed
            smoke weed Put something green
            in between but don't smoke smoke dont smoke
            hope hope hope hope Nicotine dont
            smoke the official dope
            Dope Dope Dope Dope Don't Smoke

1971; June 21, 1992

VIOLENT COLLABORATIONS

Vi-o-late me in vi-o-let times the vil-est way that you know Ru-in me Ra-vage me ut-ter-ly sa-vage me on me no mercy bes-tow

Violent Collaborations

Violate me
in violet times
the vilest way that you know
Ruin me
Ravage me
utterly savage me
on me no mercy bestow
—OLD SONG, 1944

Trespass against me
& penetrate deeply
Spare me not even your rape
Tie me up quickly
make me smile sickly
Seal up my mouth with scotch tape
—AG

Piss on me Crap on me
Wipe your fat ass on me
Make me a creature you loathe
Sorely harass me
Dont even ask me
But deal me your ultimate blow
                              —PH

Ignore me & stomp on me
Crack your big whip on me
Make me get down on my knees
Order me suck your dick
spank me & do it quick
Shove it in deep as you please
                         —AG & PH

Stun me & shun me
slave me & shave me
Give me your loathsome disease
Fuck me & fist me
in your army enlist me
Poop on me when you're at ease
                         —AG & PH

Degrade & debase me
in public deface me
come on my beard in the mud
Double me over
in summertime clover
then hose me down w/your stud
                         —AG & PH

With Peter Hale
June 1992

Calm Panic Campaign Promise

End of Millennium
                    Earth's decay—
Fire Air Water tainted
            We're the Great Beast—
                    Dark bed thoughts
Can't do anything to stop it—
Denial in Government, in Newspapers of Record—
Like watching gum disease & not brushing teeth
Getting heart failure, no rest much stress
Putting salt on your greasy pork
Putting sugar in coffee you're diabetic
            Dysesthesia on foot soles
Poor circulation smoke more cigarettes
Kick your son under the table have another beer
Need President who'll reverse the denial—
            The Calm Panic Party
            to restore nature's balance.

July 9, 1992, 12:55 A.M.

Now and Forever

I'll settle for Immortality—
Not thru the body
   Not thru the eyes
      Star-spangled high mountains
         waning moon over Aspen peaks
But thru words, thru the breath
     of long sentences
loves I have, heart beating
    still,
inspiration continuous, exhalation of
     cadenced affection
These immortal survive America,
       survive the fall of States
    Departure of my body,
      mouth dumb dust
This verse broadcasts desire,
      accomplishment of Desire
Now and forever boys can read
     girls dream, old men cry
Old women sigh
    youth still come.

July 19, 1992
Aspen

Who Eats Who?

A crow sits on the prayerflagpole,
her mate blackwinged walks the wet green grass, worms?
Yesterday seagulls skimmed the choppy waves,
    feet touching foamed breakers
                looking for salmon? halibut? sole?
Bacteria eat parameciums or vice versa,
viruses enter cells, white cell count low—
Tooth & claw on TV, lions strike down antelope—
Whales sift transparent krill thru bearded teeth.
Every cannibal niche fulfilled, Amazon
    headhunters eat testicles—
          Enemy's powers & energy become mine!

August 13, 1992
Gampo Abbey, Nova Scotia

The Charnel Ground

... rugged and raw situations, and having accepted them as
part of your home ground, then some spark of sympathy or
compassion could take place. You are not in a hurry to leave
such a place immediately. You would like to face the facts,
realities of that particular world....

FROM A COMMENTARY ON *THE SADHANA OF
MAHAMUDRA*, CHÖGYAM TRUNGPA, RINPOCHE

Upstairs Jenny crashed her car & became a living corpse, Jake sold grass,
    the white-bearded potbelly leprechaun silent climbed their
    staircase
Ex-janitor John from Poland averted his eyes, cheeks flushed with
    vodka, wine who knew what
as he left his groundfloor flat, refusing to speak to the inhabitant of
    Apt. 24
who'd put his boyfriend in Bellevue, calling police, while the artistic
    Buddhist composer
on sixth floor lay spaced out feet swollen with water, dying slowly of
    AIDS over a year—
The Chinese teacher cleaned & cooked in Apt. 23 for the homosexual
    poet who pined for his gymnast
thighs & buttocks— Downstairs th' old hippie flower girl fell drunk
    over the banister, smashed her jaw—
her son despite moderate fame cheated of rocknroll money, twenty
    thousand people in stadiums
cheering his tattooed skinhead murderous Hare Krishna vegetarian
    drum lyrics—
Mary born in the building rested on her cane, heavy-legged with heart
    failure on the second landing, no more able
to vacation in Caracas & Dublin— The Russian landlady's husband
    from concentration camp disappeared again—nobody men-
    tioned he'd died—
tenants took over her building for hot water, she couldn't add rent & pay
    taxes, wore a long coat hot days

alone & thin on the street carrying groceries to her crooked apartment
    silent—

One poet highschool teacher fell dead mysterious heart dysrhythmia,
    konked over

in his mother's Brooklyn apartment, his first baby girl a year old, wife
    stoical a few days—

their growling noisy little dog had to go, the baby cried—

Meanwhile the upstairs apartment meth head shot cocaine & yowled up
    and down

East 12th Street, kicked out of Christine's Eatery till police cornered
    him, 'top a hot iron steamhole

near Stuyvesant Town Avenue A telephone booth calling his deaf
    mother—sirens speed the way to Bellevue—

past whispering grass crack salesman jittering in circles on East 10th
    Street's

southwest corner where art yuppies come out of the overpriced Japanese
    Sushi Bar—& they poured salt into potato soup heart failure
    vats at KK's Polish restaurant

—Garbage piled up, nonbiodegradable plastic bags emptied by diabetic
    sidewalk homeless

looking for returnable bottles recycled dolls radios half-eaten
    hamburgers—thrown-away Danish—

On 13th Street the notary public sat in his dingy storefront, driver's
    lessons & tax returns prepared on old metal desks—

Sunnysides crisped in butter, fries & sugary donuts passed over the
    luncheonette counter next door—

The Hispanic lady yelled at the rude African-American behind the Post
    Office window

"I waited all week my welfare check you sent me notice I was here
    yesterday

I want to see the supervisor bitch dont insult me refusing to look in—"

Closed eyes of Puerto Rican wino lips cracked skin red stretched out

on the pavement, naphtha backdoor open for the Korean family dry
    cleaners at the 14th Street corner—

Con Ed workmen drilled all year to bust electric pipes 6 feet deep in
    brown dirt

so cars bottlenecked wait minutes to pass the M14 bus stopped mid-
road, heavy dressed senior citizens step down in red rubble
with Reduced Fare Program cards got from grey city Aging Department
offices downtown up the second flight by elevators don't
work—
News comes on the radio, they bomb Baghdad and the Garden of Eden
again?
A million starve in Sudan, mountains of eats stacked on docks, local
gangs & U.N.'s trembling bureaucrat officers sweat near the
equator arguing over
wheat piles shoved by bulldozers—Swedish doctors ran out of
medicine— The Pakistan taxi driver
says Salman Rushdie must die, insulting the Prophet in fictions—
"No that wasn't my opinion, just a character talking like in a poem no
judgment"—
"Not till the sun rejects you do I," so give you a quarter by the Catholic
church 14th St. you stand half drunk
waving a plastic glass, flush-faced, live with your mother a wounded
look on your lips, eyes squinting,
receding lower jaw sometimes you dry out in Bellevue, most days
cadging dollars for sweet wine
by the corner where Plump Blindman shifts from foot to foot showing
his white cane, rattling coins in a white paper cup some weeks
where girding the subway entrance construction sawhorses painted
orange
guard steps underground— And across the street the NYCE bank
machine cubicle door sign reads
Not in Operation as taxis bump on potholes asphalt mounded at the
crossroad when red lights change green
& I'm on my way uptown to get a CAT scan liver biopsy, visit the
cardiologist,
account for high blood pressure, kidneystones, diabetes, misty eyes &
dysesthesia—
feeling lack in feet soles, inside ankles, small of back, phallus head,
anus—
Old age sickness death again come round in the wink of an eye—

High school youth the inside skin of my thighs was silken smooth tho
     nobody touched me there back then—
Across town the velvet poet takes Darvon N, Valium nightly, sleeps all
     day kicking methadone
between brick walls sixth floor in a room cluttered with collages & gold
     dot paper scraps covered
with words: "The whole point seems to be the idea of giving away the
     giver."

August 19, 1992

Everyday

The Lama sat
    in bed
with bamboo
backscratcher
his false teeth
in a big
glass of water
on the sunny
windowsill.

August 1992

Fun House Antique Store

I'd been motoring through States &
stopped at a country antique store, an
old-fashioned house, in excellent condition—
Flower'd wallpaper, polished banisters
lampshades dusted, candelabra burnished
flaming quiet by the cloak closet
under the stairs, pitcher of water & white
washbowls beside the french doors
embroidered doilies & artificial flowers
ivory & light brown on mahogany
side tables, a brass bowl for cards,
kitchen with polished stove cold ready
at Summer's end to light up with split
wood & kindling in buckets beside
the empty fireplace, tongs & screen
in neat order. The second floor as
perfectly appointed as the foyer
(set with hat & cane rack & mirror)
stairway rugs & oaken doors, down beds
a glass-front bookcase, brown shiny bureaus,
drawers crammed with old ties & bloomers,
celluloid collars, some long-sleeved underwear, silk
& paisley shirts & shawls—and the stairs
to the third-floor attic rose five steep steps
into a blank wall nicely wallpapered with roses.
      What a delicate touch, trompe l'oeil
artistry, what charming care & magical consciousness
arranged this antique shop, so practical
for display as Bed-and-Breakfast wayfarer's
stop-over & lampshade collector's twee daydream—
Yet it was a modern commercial establishment
we'd entered casually on our own road
through Maryland to see our lawyer in D.C.—

One attendant who observed us admiring his home
appointments watched us turn to go—
I wished to make a speech: "Congratulations
on your work of Ahrt, your antique care
& delicate intelligence, as if Messrs. McDermott
& McGough photographed the 1880s entire
& built it in 3-D renewed at millennium's end—"

So I orated on but the attendants conferred,
minds elsewhere, only one scion of the house
moon-faced thirtysomething sat legs spread
on the fake stairway & applauded our appreciation
& delight—& so we left to go, our party
on its way to the postmodern Capital.

August 31, 1992

News Stays News

Diana & Roger Napoleon's real estate empire
extended up to the Napoleon Castle Hotel's penthouse
stainless steel & gold doorknobs bathtubs bars & windowsills
But Roger got Alzheimer's & couldn't keep his money books straight
Diana went to jail for back taxes & cheating at cards
Lost control of her castle, lawyers ate her Empire
She got sick & spent years maintaining her body,
skin growths, liver failure, kidney disturbances, upset stomach
But the castle of flesh ceased to function
She was left inside with her soul.
What is that? Where will it go? Who am I?
asked Napoleon in bed, eyes closing for the last time on St. Helena.

September 7, 1992, 3:00 P.M.

Autumn Leaves

At 66 just learning how to take care of my body
Wake cheerful 8 A.M. & write in a notebook
rising from bed side naked leaving a naked boy asleep by the wall
mix miso mushroom leeks & winter squash breakfast,
Check bloodsugar, clean teeth exactly, brush, toothpick, floss, mouth-
      wash
oil my feet, put on white shirt white pants white sox
sit solitary by the sink
a moment before brushing my hair, happy not yet
to be a corpse.

September 13, 1992, 9:50 A.M.

In the Benjo

To G.S.

Reading *No Nature* in the toilet
Sitting down, absorbed
    page after page, forgetting
time, forgetting my bottom
    relax, detritus
       flopping out into water
—better than pushing and squeezing,
    nervous, self-conscious—
better forget and read a book,
    let your behind take care of itself
better than hemorrhoids, a good volume
        of poetry.

October 23, 1992, 11:00 A.M.

American Sentences

Tompkins Square Lower East Side N.Y.

Four skinheads stand in the streetlight rain chatting under an umbrella.

1987

*   *   *

Bearded robots drink from Uranium coffee cups on Saturn's ring.

May 1990

*   *   *

On Hearing the Muezzin Cry Allah Akbar While Visiting the Pythian Oracle at Didyma Toward the End of the Second Millennium

At sunset Apollo's columns echo with the bawl of the One God.

*   *   *

Crescent moon, girls chatter at twilight on the busride to Ankara.

*   *   *

The weary Ambassador waits relatives late at the supper table.

*   *   *

To be sucking your thumb in Rome by the Tiber among fallen leaves . . .

June 1990

*   *   *

Rainy night on Union Square, full moon. Want more poems? Wait till I'm dead.

August 8, 1990, 3:30 A.M.

*   *   *

Approaching Seoul by Bus in Heavy Rain

Get used to your body, forget you were born, suddenly you got to get
out!

August 1990

* * *

Put on my tie in a taxi, short of breath, rushing to meditate.

November 1991
New York

* * *

Taxi ghosts at dusk pass Monoprix in Paris 20 years ago.

* * *

The young stud who dreamt I "dick'd his ass" asked me to take him to
supper.

* * *

Two blocks from his hotel in a taxi the fat Lama punched out his
mugger.

* * *

I can still see Neal's 23-year-old corpse when I come in my hand.

January 1992
Amsterdam

* * *

Naropa Hot Tub

The ocean is full of naked young boys and Neptune-bearded old men.

July 1992

*   *   *

He stands at the church steps a long time looking down at new white
     sneakers—
Determined, goes in the door quickly to make his Sunday confession.

September 21, 1992

*   *   *

The midget albino entered the hairy limousine to pipi.

September 25, 1992
Modesto

*   *   *

That grey-haired man in business suit and black turtleneck thinks he's
     still young.

December 19, 1992

NOTES

These reference notes may be of use to younger readers & translators not familiar with ephemeral news situations or translated & esoteric texts.

Title page epigraph
Section 2, "Discussion on Making All Things Equal," *Chuang Tzu Basic Writings*, trans. Burton Watson (New York: Columbia University Press, 1964), p. 42.

(p. xiii) *Improvisation in Beijing*
Discourse at Chinese Writers Association conference with American Academy of Arts and Letters on "Sources of Inspiration," Beijing, October 1984. Improvised from notes, transcribed from tape, lightly edited.

(p. xvii) *Prologue: Visiting Father & Friends*
See "At the Grave of My Father," Louis Ginsberg, *Collected Poems*, ed. Michael Fournier, Introduction Eugene Brooks, Afterword Allen Ginsberg (Orono, Maine: Northern Lights, 1992).

(p. 5) *On the Conduct of the World*
Roque Dalton: Salvadorian poet-hero-martyr (1935–1975) was liquidated by fellow FMLN revolutionists for tactical differences of opinion.

Velemir Khlebnikov (1885–1922), *Snake Train* (Ann Arbor: Ardis House, 1976). The classic Futurist poet perished after returning by train from Pyatigorsk to Moscow, "weakened by malnutrition and repeated bouts of typhus and malaria." See *The King of Time, Selected Writings of the Russian Futurian*, trans. Paul Schmidt (Cambridge: Harvard University Press, 1983).

(p. 9) *Spot Anger*
"Drive All Blames into One"—i.e., oneself. Jamgon Kongtrul, *The Great Path of Awakening. A Commentary on the Mahayana Teaching of the Seven Points of Mind Training*, trans. Ken McLeod (Boston: Shambhala Press, 1987). Original text by Atisa.

(p. 10) *London Dream Doors*
"God sent him to sea for pearls": "For in my nature I quested for beauty, but God, God hath sent me to sea for pearls." Christopher Smart, *Jubilate Agno*, ed. W. H. Bond (New York: Greenwood Press, 1969).

(p. 12) *Cosmopolitan Greetings*
Response to Macedonian request for message to Struga Evenings of Poetry festival, on receiving 1986 Golden Laurel Wreath prize.
"Molecule/clinking against molecule.": See "Winter Night," *Attila József's Selected Poems and Texts*, trans. John Bátki (Iowa City: International Writing Program, University of Iowa, 1976).
First Thought, Best Thought, Chögyam Trungpa (Boston: Shambhala Press, 1984).
"If the mind is shapely, the art will be shapely": Jack Kerouac and Allen Ginsberg, conversation 1958, Cherry Plains, N.Y.

(p. 15) *Fifth Internationale*
See the "Internationale," former Soviet national anthem:
"Arise ye prisoners of starvation,
Arise ye wretched of the earth,
For justice thunders condemnation,
A better world's in birth," etc.
Crazy Wisdom: i.e., wild wisdom "whispered lineage," characteristic of Kagyu school, Tibetan Buddhism. See Chögyam Trungpa, Rinpoche, *Crazy Wisdom* (Boston: Shambhala Press, 1992).

(p. 17) *Europe, Who Knows?*
Russian *Chernobyl* translates literally as "wormwood."

(p. 18) *"Graphic Winces"*
Collaboration with Brooklyn College M.F.A. Writing Workshop, Fall 1986, and Bob Rosenthal.

(p. 19) *Imitation of K.S.*
Jack Micheline, *Skinny Dynamite* (San Francisco: Second Coming Press, 1980). Story by the poet-painter.

(p. 25) *On Cremation of Chögyam Trungpa*
Cremation ceremony took place at Karme-Chöling Retreat Center, Barnet, Vermont.

(p. 27) *Nanao*
Written for back jacket copy, *Break the Mirror: The Poems of Nanao Sakaki* (San Francisco: North Point Press, 1987).

(p. 34) *Salutations to Fernando Pessoa*

See "Salutation to Walt Whitman," *The Poems of Fernando Pessoa*, trans. Edwin Honig and Susan M. Brown (New York: Ecco Press, 1987).

(p. 37) *May Days 1988*

"Arabs should throw words not stones," Elie Wiesel, quoted in *New York Post* sometime 1988.

(p. 42) *Return of Kral Majales*

See "Kral Majales," p. 353 and notes, *Collected Poems 1947–1980* (New York: Harper & Row, 1984).

Sen. Jesse Helms & Heritage Foundation's October 1988 law directed Federal Communications Commission to enforce 24-hour ban on "indecent" language over all airwaves, declared unconstitutional by subsequent court decisions. At poem's writing, ban extended 6:00 A.M. to midnight. Court decisions 1993 froze ban as of 6:00 A.M. to 8:00 P.M., leaving as "safe harbor" late evening to 6:00 A.M. Daytime broadcast for students (& adults) reading the author's "questionable" poems in schools is now forbidden by law.

All gone all gone . . .: version of *Prajnaparamita*, Highest Perfect Wisdom, 17-syllable Sanskrit mantra: "Gate Gate Paragate Parasamgate Bodhi Svaha."

(p. 43) *Elephant in the Meditation Hall*

"As late as 1988, 333 House members and 61 Senators hosted significant donations from Savings & Loan lobbyists." "S & L Scandal: The Gang's all Here," by Mary Fricher and Steve Pizzo, *New York Times* Op-Ed, July 27, 1990.

(p. 49) *Poem in the Form of a Snake That Bites Its Tail*

Ojus: hard coral limestone formations, North Miami area, Florida.

(p. 55) *CIA Dope Calypso*

See *New York Times*, March 12, 1989:

HULL BAILED OUT IN COSTA RICA

San Jose, Costa Rica, March 10 (AP)—American-born John Hull, who has been linked to Nicaraguan rebel supply network, was released from prison Friday after he posted $37,000 bail, his attorney said. The 69-year-old Mr. Hull, who was jailed on Jan. 13 on charges of drug trafficking and violating Costa Rican security, was freed soon after friends collected bail money. Mr. Hull has lived in Costa Rica for 20 years. He is accused of allowing his ranch to be used by the Nicaraguan contras and of narcotics trafficking between 1982–1985.

Part I originally published in *First Blues* (New York: Full Court Press, 1979). Here two additional sections update events. For scholarly history of government intelligence involvement with drug trafficking to aid or fund "off-the-shelf" secret & illegal operations, including most references in "CIA Dope Calypso," see Alfred McCoy, *The Politics of Heroin* (Brooklyn: Lawrence Hill Books, 1991), to which poet contributed research.

(p. 60) *Just Say Yes Calypso*

After aiding CIA overthrow of Iran's legal Premier Mohammed Mossadegh, General N. Schwarzkopf's father, Norman Schwarzkopf, Sr., trained the Shah's dreaded secret police, the Savak. See "Capitol Air," *Collected Poems 1947–1980; Lies of Our Times*, vol. 2, no. 2 (February 19, 1991) (New York: Sheridan Square Press); and James Breslin, "A Son Follows Suit in the Matter of Oil," *New York Newsday*, September 9, 1990.

(p. 62) *Hum Bom!*

Part I and shorter version of Part II were published in *Collected Poems 1947–1980*. Additional verses added 1991.

(p. 69) *Big Eats*

Mahamudra poetics exercise suggested by Khenpo Tsultrim Gyamtso, Rinpoche, Rocky Mountain Dharma Center, Summer 1991. The first of five verses, 21 syllables each, begins in "neurotic confusion" (Samsara), the last concludes grounded in "ordinary mind" (Dharmakaya).

(p. 77) *After Lalon*

Lalon Shah (1774–1890), Bengali Baul singer, devotional forerunner of Rabindranath Tagore. See *Songs of Lalon Shah*, trans. Abu Rushd (Dhaka: Bangla Academy Press, 1991).

(p. 82) *Get It?*

Verse 1: Ref. Rodney King videotape beating and police trials, Los Angeles 1992–93.

Verse 3: Ref. Police frame-up of political poet Amiri Baraka, 1966, later thrown out of court.

Verse 4: Ref. J. Edgar Hoover's amative relationship with assistant

Clyde Tolson and his withholding of Kennedy assassination information from Warren Commission. See Curt Gentry, *J. Edgar Hoover: The Man and His Secrets* (New York: Penguin, 1991); and Anthony Summers, *Official and Confidential: The Secret Life of J. Edgar Hoover* (New York: Putnam, 1993).

Verse 5: Ref. Oswald's role as government intelligence informant within Fair Play for Cuba Committee.

Verse 6: Ref. Jack Ruby, courier to Cuba for Mafioso boss Santos Trafficante, Jr., former drug lord of Havana.

Verse 7: See "N.S.A. Dope Calypso" pp. 58–59, stanzas 3–6, and note.

Verse 8: Ref. Oliver North, Richard Secord, etc.

Verse 9: Ref. Elliott Abrams, former Assistant Secretary of State for Latin America, pardoned by outgoing President Bush 1992 after guilty plea to withholding Iran–contra scam information from Congress.

Verse 13: Charles H. Keating, Jr., 69, founder, Cincinnati Citizens for Decent Literature, later Citizens for Decency Through Law, was convicted 1993 on state and federal charges of swindling investors, fraud, and racketeering in collapse of Lincoln Savings and Loan Association. "The collapse of Lincoln, which was based in Irvine, California, in early 1989 is estimated to have cost taxpayers $2.5 billion" (*New York Times*, September 4, 1992). Along with pedophile Father Joseph Ritter, former director of wayward youths' Covenant House, Keating was outstanding homophobe on President Reagan's Meese Commission on Pornography.

(p. 84) *Research*

Verse 6: Rev. W. A. Criswell, mentor of TV Bible evangelist fund-raising theopoliticians Jimmy Swaggart, Pat Robertson, Jerry Falwell, and Billy Graham, decrees the Bible 100 percent "Inerrant."

Verse 11: John Rousas Rushdoony, fundamentalist author, leader of Chalcedon Foundation's Christian Reconstructionist exertions, disapproves homosexual emotions.

(p. 87) *Put Down Your Cigarette Rag*

Originally published in *First Blues* (New York: Full Court Press, 1975). Here updated statistics, additional stanzas.

(p. 91) *Violent Collaborations*

Epigraph remembered from 1940s college days, heard by classmate from his mother, perhaps 1920s flappers' ditty.

(p. 96) *The Charnel Ground*

Epigraph and final quotation, "The whole point seems to be the idea of giving away the giver," taken from lectures on *The Sadhana of Mahamudra*, by Ven. Chögyam Trungpa, Rinpoche, Karma Dzong, December 1973, privately printed.

(p. 105) *In the Benjo*

Gary Snyder, *No Nature: New and Selected Poems* (New York: Pantheon, 1992).

(p. 106) *American Sentences*

On Hearing the Muezzin Cry Allah Akbar While Visiting the Pythian Oracle at Didyma Toward the End of the Second Millennium

Didyma, Asia Minor's shore site where Magna Màter and Pythian oracle were displaced by Judeo-Christian-Islamic Father God. In response to imperial Roman request for prophecy circa 4th century A.D., the oracle's last utterance declared the gods had departed, Apollo no longer inhabited the temple's pillars.

Rainy night on Union Square . . . Answering office mail late night, response to request from little magazine.

(p. 107) *Approaching Seoul by Bus in Heavy Rain*

Bus over steep mountains from Kangnung to Seoul one rainy night was delayed along precipice by a mile of ambulance lights marking crash of bus I'd missed, scheduled an hour earlier.

Monoprix, familiar department store, onetime right bank of Seine across from Place St. Michel.

INDEX OF TITLES AND FIRST LINES
(*Titles are in italics*)